A Book of Love for

My
Daughter

September 19, 2001

To my fabulous
Krissi.

I love you!

xoxo
mama

A Book of Love for *My* *Daughter*

H. Jackson Brown, Jr., Paula Y. Flautt, and Kim Shea

RUTLEDGE HILL PRESS®
Nashville, Tennessee

A THOMAS NELSON COMPANY

Published by Rutledge Hill Press, a Thomas Nelson company, P.O. Box 141000, Nashville, Tennessee 37214.

Pages 8–9; 91–94; 122–123 from *Butterfly Kisses and Bittersweet Tears* by Bob Carlisle. Copyright © 1998 by Bob Carlisle. Published by Word Publishing, Nashville, Tennessee. All rights reserved.

Pages 18–19; 119–120 from *Rainbows Live at Easter* by Gloria Gaither. Copyright © 1974 by Gloria Gaither. Used by permission.

Pages 22–23 from *When God Whispers Your Name* by Max Lucado. Copyright © 1994, 1999 by Max Lucado. Published by Word Publishing, Nashville, Tennessee. All rights reserved.

Pages 27–19; 57–59 from *Different Roads* by Kathy Troccoli. Copyright © 1999 by Kathy Troccoli. Published by Word Publishing, Nashville, Tennessee. All rights reserved.

Pages 31–32; 62–65 from *A Man Called Daddy* by Hugh O'Neill. Copyright © 1996 by Hugh O'Neill. Published by Rutledge Hill Press, Nashville, Tennessee. All rights reserved.

Pages 34–35 from *Sitting by My Laughing Fire* by Ruth Bell Graham. Copyright © 1977 by Ruth Bell Graham. Used by permission.

Pages 39–41 from *The Gift of a Child* by Marion Stroud. Copyright © 1982 by Marion Stroud. Used by permission.

Pages 70–72 from *See You at the House* by Bob Benson. Copyright © 1986 by Peggy Benson. Courtesy of Deeper Life Ministries, Nashville, Tennessee. Used by permission.

Pages 84–87 from *Friends Through Thick and Thin* by Gloria Gaither, Peggy Benson, Sue Buchanan, and Joy MacKenzie. Copyright © 1998 by Gloria Gaither, Peggy Benson, Sue Buchanan, and Joy MacKenzie. Used by permission.

Pages 96–97; 116 from *A Song for Sarah* by Paula D'Arcy. Copyright © 1979, revised 1995 by Paula D'Arcy. Published by WaterBrook Press, Colorado Springs, Colorado. All rights reserved.

Pages 99–101 from *The Applause from Heaven* by Max Lucado. Copyright © 1999 by Max Lucado. Published by Word Publishing, Nashville, Tennessee. All rights reserved.

Pages 105–107 from Mary Beth Chapman. Used by permission.

Pages 110–114 from *Laughter in the Walls* by Bob Benson. Copyright © 1969, 1996 by Peggy Benson. Used by permission.

Pages 218; 247; 274–275 from *A Daily Dose of the American Dream* by Alan C. Elliott. Copyright © 1998 by Alan C. Elliott. Published by Rutledge Hill Press, Nashville, Tennessee. All rights reserved.

Cover and text design by Gore Studios.

Library of Congress Cataloging in Publication data available.

ISBN 1-55853-866-6

Printed in the United States of America

1 2 3 4 5 6 7 8 9—06 05 04 03 02 01

CONTENTS

OTHER BOOKS BY H. JACKSON BROWN, JR.

A Father's Book of Wisdom

P.S. I Love You

Life's Little Instruction Book™ (volumes I, II, and III)

Live and Learn and Pass It On (volumes I, II, and III)

Wit and Wisdom from the Peanut Butter Gang

The Little Book of Christmas Joys
   (with Rosemary C. Brown and Kathy Peel)

A Hero in Every Heart (with Robyn Spizman)

Life's Little Treasure Books
   On Marriage and Family, On Wisdom, On Joy
   On Success, On Love, On Parenting, Of Christmas Memories,
   Of Christmas Traditions, On Hope, On Friendship, On Fathers,
   On Mothers, On Things That Really Matter, On Simple Pleasures

Kids' Little Treasure Books
   On Happy Families
   On What We've Learned . . . So Far

Life's Little Instructions from the Bible (with Rosemary C. Brown)

Life's Little Instruction Book™ for Incurable Romantics (with Robyn
   Spizman)

Life's Little Instruction Book™ for Mothers to Daughters (with Kim Shea)

A Book of Love for My Son (with Hy Brett)

Remembrances

Compiled by Paula Y. Flautt

It has been the blessing of my life to have been loved well as a daughter. I have been believed in, encouraged, challenged, supported, nurtured, and celebrated. It has been through these things—my parents' love for me as their daughter—that I learned what it means to love the daughters given to me; to treasure their chance to live their lives, their choices, their dreams; to savor the moments between us; to give myself and rejoice in their "selves"!

Every morning when I went in to take my oldest daughter from her crib, I felt like I was opening the most wonderful Christmas present that could ever be! Every night when she'd wake up to be nursed and rocked back to sleep was an incredible, special, secret time between just us. Those moments, and so many more, with her and her sister have, for the last eighteen years, been a source of delight and joy every one of my days.

It is my hope that this book—this collection of remembrances, instructions, and dreams—will in some way be a source of delight and joy for you; that it will encourage you, inspire you; that it will trigger your own memories within and that perhaps one day will be something for you to share with a daughter of your own.

— Paula Y. Flautt
January 2000

*O*h, my son's my son till he gets him a wife,
But my daughter's my daughter all her life.

— Dinah Maria Mulock Crakik

A little girl, asked where her home was, replied, "where mother is."

— Keith L. Brooks

*Y*es, the race of children possesses magically sagacious powers!

— Gail Godwin

Sweet bud of promise, fresh and fair
Just moving in the morning air.
The morn of life but just begun,
The sands of time just set to run!

Sweet babe with cheek of pinky hue,
With eyes of soft ethereal blue,
With raven hair like finest down
Of unfledged bird, and scant'ly shown
Beneath the cap of cumbrous lace,
And circles round thy placid face!

Ah, baby! Little dost thou know
How many yearning bosoms glow,
How many lips in blessings move,
How many eyes beam looks of love
At sight of thee!

— Joanna Baillie

February 14, 1983

$\mathcal{M}$y Darling Curry, you are six days away from being seventeen months old. It is Valentine's Day and so appropriate for me to begin this journal, for you are my special valentine!

How can I tell you in words what you mean? How I love you? When you were first born I would go in to get you in the early hours; it was like Christmas morning every day . . . and you were the most wonderous present.

—Paula Y. Flautt, Journal for My Daughters

Pink Roses

*W*hen I was seventeen and a senior in high school, my dad's company transferred him to a different state. It was a blow to our family. Although Dad wasn't one to say a lot about his feelings, he was always really good to me, and I knew being away from us was really hard on him.

On my eighteenth birthday, he was in New York. Although he tried to phone a couple of times, I never got the messages. It wasn't a particularly happy day for me because of some things that went wrong at school. But the worst of it was that Dad wasn't there on my birthday.

The next morning he called the house before I left for school. When he wished me a happy birthday and asked me how my day had gone, I started crying and couldn't stop. Finally I just told him, "I had a terrible day, and I wish you'd been here."

That afternoon, I was called out of class and asked to report to the school office. When I got there, I found that a dozen pink roses had been delivered to me. When I read the card, I started crying all over again. It said, "I love you, Dad"

Like I said before, Dad isn't one to express his feelings. But when he does, he means it. And on that day, I heard him loud and clear.

— S. B., Atlanta, Ga. (from *Butterfly Kisses & Bittersweet Tears,* by Bob Carlisle)

She discovered with great delight that one does not love one's children just because they are one's children but because of the friendship formed while raising them.

— Gabriel Garcia Marquez

Oh, for those young embroiderers of bygone days, sitting on hard little stools in the shelter of their mother's ample skirts! Maternal authority kept them there for years and years, never rising except to change the skein of silk or to elope with a stranger.

— Colette

It's a Mother Thing

She was perfect! That's what I thought when I first saw my only daughter, Leigh, right after she was born. A tiny, lovely, six-pound bundle of pink humanity! I remember thinking, "There is no way I'll ever be this happy again." I thought myself a most fortunate mother, and I felt that I could never love her more than I did at that moment. But was I ever wrong! I have discovered through the years, I love and respect her more with each day that passes.

Don't let me mislead you. We have had our share of differences, especially concerning "important stuff" like clothes, makeup, hairstyles, her choice of friends, and the boys in her life.

There have been days so full of laughter and joy that I couldn't begin to express the flood of overwhelming love I had for her in my heart. There have been nights of the soul when our relationship was cold and unfriendly and lonely; we felt hurt and out of touch with each other. I wondered during those times if we would ever really be friends.

But we have become friends, and what a delight she has been in my life. I have watched this lovely person grow and blossom into a fine young woman. She is a wife, a mother, and a homemaker, an artist, a writer, and a pastor to children. Like most mothers I know, she has managed to stretch herself in so many directions, there isn't much time left for herself. Leigh is basically a giver. She knows how to give her heart and her ears to listen to the lives of others.

I must admit the word *listening* has never been tops on my priority list of words. I have always been a talker. Somehow I have had the idea that talking was something you did while you thought about what you should be saying! Bob used to say (teasing me, I think!) that I should learn to knit, so I would have something to think about while I talked. Leigh, on the other hand, is good at listening. By nature, she is shy, quiet, and soft-spoken. She doesn't enjoy publicity or calling attention to herself.

Whether baking cookies with her two young children, or planting a wildflower garden, or sharing a picnic on a warm summer day— she gets to practice her listening skills quite a bit, since it turns out both of her children are big talkers. She has let me know—in a tactful way, of course—she believes they inherited their need to converse constantly from their maternal grandmother.

Britt and Annie talk to big people, little people, elderly people—all people. As Leigh often has said, they force people to be open and friendly! At the end of the day, she tries to save enough energy to hear her husband, as he shares his hopes and dreams for their life together. Occasionally, she still counsels with her four brothers, for whom she has served as "vice-mother" (a name given her by her father during her growing up years). She offers them emotional support and never, ever betrays their confidence. Finally, she takes time to allow her mother the use of her ear as a sounding board to work through the problems that arise from being alone. In many ways, we have begun the process of role reversal. She is becoming the mother, and I the daughter. (Growing up is overrated anyway!)

Not too long ago, as she was leaving my house to make the trip back to the farm where she and her family live and I was helping her put the babies in the car, she said to me, with a lilt in her voice, "Mom, I did something this morning that was so much like you, it scared me." We laughed at the idea of that, and as I watched her pull away I thought about what she'd said. It occurred to me that in a humorous way, she might be saying that she thought she hadn't always met my expectations for her—expectations that might include being like me.

If I am totally honest, I must admit, I would be pleased for people to say I was like her! She is, at thirty-six, a long way ahead of what I was at her age. She possesses qualities and strengths and a resiliency that I have worked all my life to own. I hope she knows from my words and actions that she is more than I dreamed possible.

That little girl that was put in my arms all those years ago, the one who used to tug at my apron strings now tugs at my heartstrings. I have come to realize this tug never goes away. It's a mother thing, and I'm tied to her for life!

— Peggy Benson

I was always glad that I was a girl. As a girl, I knew that someday I would have children. My closest models, my mother and my grandmother, had both children and a career. So I had no doubt that whatever career I might choose, I would have children too.

— Margaret Mead

Christmas, 1986

$\mathcal{D}$arling Anna . . . the sweetest part of Christmas was rocking you to sleep!

—Paula Y. Flautt, Journal for my Daughters

Value

You came and you took.
You took time
And energy
And time
And attention
And time
And love
And time
And elbow grease
And time
And my sleep
And time.

But you brought more.
You brought sunshine
And bubbles
And music
And laughter
And sandboxes
And playdough
And yellow ribbons

And flesh-colored Bandaids
And arpeggio scales
And "The Waltons"
And roller skates
And blow-up kites
And Joy.
You were the best investment I ever made.

— Gloria Gaither

*B*eing a daughter is only half the equation; bearing one is the other.

— Erica Jong

*I*n the final analysis it is not what you do for your children but what you have taught them to do for themselves that will make them successful human beings.

— Ann Landers

*A*ll children, except one, grow up. They soon know that they will grow up, and the way Wendy knew was this. One day when she was two years old she was playing in a garden, and she plucked another flower and ran with it to her mother. I supposed she must have looked rather delightful, for Mrs. Darling put her hand to her heart and cried, "Oh, why can't you remain like this for ever!"

— James Barrie, from *Peter Pan*

$\mathcal{T}rust$

$\mathcal{I}$ stand six steps from the bed's edge. My arms extended. Hands open. On the bed, Sara—all four years of her—crouches, poised like a playful kitten. She's going to jump. But she's not ready. I'm too close.

"Back more, Daddy," she stands and dares.

I dramatically comply, confessing admiration for her courage. After two giant steps I stop. "More?" I ask.

"Yes!" Sara squeals, hopping on the bed.

With each step she laughs and claps and motions for more. When I'm on the other side of the canyon, when I'm on the horizon, she stops me. "There, stop there."

"Are you sure?"

"I'm sure," she shouts. I extend my arms. Once again she crouches, then springs. Superman without a cape. Skydiver without a chute. Only her heart flies higher than her body. In that airborne instant her only hope is her father. If he proves weak, she'll fall. If he proves cruel, she'll crash. If he proves forgetful, she'll tumble to the hard floor.

But such fear she does not know, for her father she does. She trusts him. Four years under the same roof have convinced her he is reliable. He is no superhuman, but he is strong. He is not holy, but he is good. He's not brilliant, but he doesn't have to remember to catch his child when she jumps.

And so she flies.

And so she soars.

And so he catches her and the two rejoice at the wedding of her trust and his faithfulness.

— Max Lucado

To Thee O God alone be praise
And thanks to Thee for grace,
That Thou has vouchsafed to me
To look on Katherine's face.

The jewels she wears are godliness.
She helps me bear my cross.
She will have reward of Thee.
She counts the world but dross.

— Elisabeth of Braunschweig

Childhood is the kingdom where nobody dies.

— Edna St. Vincent Millay

The arbitrary divisions of one's life into weeks and days and hours seemed, on the whole, useless. There was but one day for the men, and that was pay day, and one for the women, and that was rent day. As for the children, every day was theirs, just as it should be in every corner of the world.

— Alice Caldwell Rice

June 4, 1992

An afternoon and night of "just us" time. . . . We shopped. . . .
You always like to cook, so when we came home we (you) baked a cake.
I had white icing, but you wanted colored. I had blue, yellow, and green
food coloring. "Which one?" I said. "All of them" you said, "I might want
to make a rainbow cake!" So you made a patchwork cake and then deco-
rated it with all the kinds of sprinkles in the house. After eating cake we
sat down to read—me a page and you a page—a storybook and then
your bible book. The story was about Zacchaeus and Jesus coming to his
house. I teased and said "Imagine if Jesus told you he was coming to
your house! You'd have to run home and clean up your room. You
looked up at me and said, "I don't think Jesus would mind."

—Paula Y. Flautt, Journal for My Daughters

God Designed This Road for Me

Upon graduating from college, I began climbing the corporate ladder in an international costume jewelry company. At age twenty-nine, I was one step away from the highest position in the company. I was responsible for thirty-seven employees—most of whom were old enough to be my father—and one training director. My salary increased to six figures. My husband and I were living the proverbial good life . . . but something was missing.

Gradually, my desire to scale the next hurdle diminished, and I found myself yearning for something—rather someone—I had never thought about: a baby. These new feelings were fleeting but real. They would peak when a co-worker became pregnant or a friend gave birth.

It wasn't long before the desire for motherhood became overwhelming.

It took about three years for me to acknowledge God's plan. During that time I suffered from mental fatigue and from something much, much worse—the anguish of two miscarriages and the despair of infertility. After enduring countless tests and fertility drugs, I began to believe I would never have a child. I prayed more and slept less.

When my best friend became pregnant, I was ecstatic for her but heartbroken for my own empty arms. . . . "Haven't you heard my prayers God?" I sat and wept. Suddenly a still small voice spoke to my heart the word *Ruth*. Immediately, my spirit understood. I ran to my bible and the verse I was drawn to took my breath away: "And no my daughter, don't be afraid. I will do for you all you ask. . . ."

God had heard my prayer! Someday I would be a mother!

My husband and I used the promises from God's word to silence the doubts of doctors and loved ones . . . we prayed fervently . . . I began to anticipate the day I would hold a baby in my arms.

What a joy filled our hearts a year and a half later when . . . Nicholas Robert Gardner came into the world . . . Less than three years later our daughter was born, and right now we are expecting our third child.

The road I chose for myself almost ten years ago is unrecognizable to me now. The road God has designed for me to walk is more challenging than anything I encountered in the business world—and much more fulfilling. I'm so thankful He . . . allowed me to be a mother.

— Donna Gardner

*H*er little girl was late arriving home from school, so that mother began to scold her:

"Why are you so late?"

"I had to help another girl. She was in trouble."

"What did you do to help her?"

"Oh, I sat down and helped her cry."

— Anonymous

*M*ama exhorted her children at every opportunity to "jump at de sun. "We might not land on the sun, but at least we would get off the ground.

— Zora Neale Hurston

Daddy Can Sing

Here's the best thing about having children. I love to sing. And like most folks, when I'm in the shower, I let 'er rip. I do Sinatra, Springsteen. I have both a Whitney Houston medley and packed-house fantasies. But alas, the fantasies are all I have. I can't sing at all.

Don't try telling that to Rebecca.

The four of us were cruising along in the car, James Taylor on the tape player. When a elegiac song called "The Water Is Wide" began, I joined in with Sweet Baby James. And the truth is with Mudslide Slim as backup, some plaintive violins, and a little orchestration, I held my own.

The car got suddenly quiet, the way a theater does in magic moments. When the song ended, there was a an extra beat of that silence and then Rebecca, clearly moved, said through a sniffle, "Daddy, that was beautiful." I got credit for it all. Words, music, arrangement, performance.

And now, every time Rebecca and I go anywhere in the care, she pops in that tape and asks me to sing "The Water Is Wide." She doesn't want to hear James Taylor. She wants to hear me. When the song is over, she looks at me in this admiring way, as though it's just splendid the world has such talent in it.

Rebecca has lots of wonderful opinions. She also thinks I'm strong, smart, funny, and tall. She makes me feel a little of each. F. Scott Fitzgerald once wrote that the greatest gift was to be perceived exactly the way you wished to be. Hallelujah and God bless her! My daughter thinks Daddy can sing!

—Hugh O'Neill, *A Man Called Daddy*

For unflagging interest and enjoyment, a household of children,
if things go reasonably well, certainly makes all other forms of
success and achievement lose their importance by comparison.

—Theodore Roosevelt

Like a round loaf . . .
I kneaded you, patted you,
Greased you smooth, floured you.

— Judith Toth

*I*t seems but yesterday
you lay
new in my arms.
into our lives you brought
sunshine
and laughter—
play—
showers, too,
and song.

Headstrong,
heartstrong,
gay,
tender beyond believing,
simple in faith,
clear-eyed,

shy,
eager for life—
you left us
rich in memories,
little wife.
And now today
I hear you say
words wise beyond your years;
I watch you play
with your small son,
tenderest of mothers.
Years slip away—

today
we are mothers
Together.

— Ruth Bell Graham

August 14, 1995

You kissed me at bedtime and said, "Mom, you're my best friend. . . ." Those were some of the dearest words I've ever heard.

—Paula Y. Flautt, Journal for My Daughters

Who would ever think that so much can go on in the soul of a young girl?

— Anne Frank

What feeling is so nice as a child's hand in yours? So small, so soft and warm, like a kitten huddling in the shelter of your clasp.

— Marjorie Holmes

In youth time flies upon a silken wing.

— Katharine Augusta Ware

Daddy said] "All children must look after their own upbringing." Parents can only give good advice or put them on the right paths, but the final forming of a person's character lies in their own hands.

—Anne Frank

The first thing a child should learn is how to endure. It is what he will have most need to know.

— Jean-Jacques Rousseau

Love Is

Love is . . . pacing the floor through the hours
  after midnight,
  soothing your crying with love-words and lullabies,
  when all of my being is begging for rest.

Love is . . . a painting of a scarlet giant with no arms and a
single eye, bearing that heart-stopping legend in
  wobbly letters: 'My Mommy is Best.'

Love is . . . reading the same story for the sixth night
  running and not missing any of it out.

Love is . . . the last sticky sweet in the bag, only slightly
    licked and faintly dusted with dirt and dog-hairs,
    resolutely not eaten, because you had decided to keep
    it for me.

Love is . . . learning new skills so that we can help you to develop
    yours.

Love is . . . cold coffee and a soggy roll placed tenderly by
    our bed at 6:30 A.M., so that I don't have to get up
    early on my birthday.

Love is . . . caring enough to say 'no,' even if 'everybody else is
    doing it.'

Love is . . . letting you go with a lump in my throat, a
prayer in my heart and a smile on my face, as you
stride out of the door to take on the world.

Love is . . . struggling to share the faith that is our sure
foundation, so that you, a child of the present, can
have a light for the future.

— Marion Stroud

June 22, 1992

$\mathcal{T}$he best of days! We went to Cheekwood, one of your favorite places. We picnicked, read *Alice in Wonderland* aloud, fed the huge carp in the pond, and explored the Red Grooms exhibit. . . . As we sketched in the gardens you said, "Don't you just love the word *summer?*"

—Paula Y. Flautt, Journal for My Daughters

What images return
Oh my daughter . . .

—T.S. Eliot

A child is a person who is going to carry on what you have
started . . . the fate of humanity is in his hands.

—Abraham Lincoln

Who will tell me how my daughter appears to herself?

— Colette

$\mathscr{I}$t is admirable for a man to take his son fishing, but there is a special place in heaven for the father who takes his daughter shopping.

— John Sinor

$\mathscr{W}$hat do girls do who haven't any mothers to help them through their troubles?

— Louisa May Alcott

*H*e that would the daughter win, Must with the mother first begin.

— English proverb

*E*veryone can keep house better than her mother, until she tries.

—Thomas Fuller

*T*here's no place like home. There's no place like home.

— Dorothy
(from *The Wonderful Wizard of Oz*)

$\mathcal{I}$t is not possible for civilization to flow backward while there is youth in the world. Youth may be headstrong, but it will advance its allotted length.

— Helen Keller

$\mathcal{C}$hildren sweeten labours.

— Francis Bacon

"$\mathcal{F}$lowers o' the home," says he, "are daughters."

— Marceline Desbordes-Valmore

April 30, 1995

*L*ast night was the final show of *A Midsummer Night's Dream.* From the time I started working on this show you were dreaming up ways to be in it! I wanted to be sure I wasn't just finagling a way for you to be in it, so I held out casting you. Then, in a flash at a rehearsal, I saw I needed little night creatures creeping out of the dark to watch Titania sleep. . . . With your large gossamer wings, you creeped and fluttered . . . you did well both onstage and off (during the strike)! Oh, how I love you my beautiful butterfly!

—Paula Y. Flautt, Journal for My Daughters

There are little coats and caps and hoods
Around our house these days,
There are little dresses, gowns and shirts
For which a father pays!
But somehow of the things there are
That little babies use,
I seem to notice most of all
Her little soft-sole shoes.

I see them every night there on the bench,
Atop her pile of clothes,
Like little boats a-riding waves
A pleasant sea-wind blows,

And yet not boats out on the deep,
For in the toes there wink
At me some quite big holes would make
Them fill with sea and sink.

I pick them up and muse a while,
I turn them up and down,
Those little boots of buttoned-black
With soles so soft and brown.
Much nearer do they come to me
Than anything she wears,
They seem to solemnize my thoughts
And call me to my prayers.

I wonder why they lure me so,

What power do they possess

To make a strong man stand and dream?

I cannot even guess,

But somehow of the things she has,

That little babies use,

I love and cherish most of all

Those little soft-sole shoes.

—— Barton Rees Pogue

A child is not a vase to be filled, but a fire to be lit.

— Francois Rabelais

. . . the passionate belief in the superior worthwhileness of our children. It is stored up in us as a great battery charged by the accumulated instincts of uncounted generations.

— Ruth Benedict

*M*onday's child is fair of face,

Tuesday's child is full of grace,

Wednesday's child is full of woe,

Thursday's child has far to go,

Friday's child is loving and giving,

Saturday's child has to work for its living

But a child that's born on the Sabbath day

Is fair and wise and good and gay.

—Anonymous

December, 1995

We were finishing decorating the tree. . . you had hung all the largest and nicest angels up near the angel on the top. Not the way I wanted . . . and then you said . . . "*This* is the heavenly host!"

—Paula Y. Flautt, Journal for My Daughters

The Lovable Child

Frisky as a lambkin,
Busy as a bee—
That's the kind of little girl people like to see.

Modest as a violet,
As a rosebud sweet—
That's the kind of little girl
People like to meet.

Bright as a diamond
Pure as any pearl—
Everyone rejoices in
Such a little girl.

Happy as a robin
Gentle as a dove—
That's the kind of little girl
Everyone will love.

Fly away and seek her,
Little song of mine,
For I choose that very girl
As my valentine.

— Emilie Poulsson

$\mathcal{Y}$outh is, after all, just a moment, but it is the moment, the spark that you always carry in your heart.

— Raisa M. Gorbachev

$\mathcal{W}$here, oh where are the children? . . .
That lovely voice; how I should weep for joy if I could hear it now!

— Colette

$\mathcal{P}$retty much all the honest truthtelling there is in the world is done by children.

— Oliver Wendell Holmes

The Road I Never Planned To Take

Life was going pretty much according to our plan. We had been married three years when our daughter Holly, came into our lives. What a joy she was to us.

Then three years later another baby was on the way, and Jim and I were thrilled. As the weeks and months passed our anticipation grew. Would it be a boy or a girl?

Finally, in the early morning hours of August twenty-fourth, two weeks past her due date, Shelly Anne came into our lives. We now had two little girls. We both rejoiced at what God had done for us.

Then word came from the doctors—our baby girl had multiple problems. We spent New Year's Eve in the emergency room where Shelly's life hung in the balance . . . and that was just the beginning. She was unable to sit up, exhibited some mental retardation, had speech problems, and on and on the list went. This was not the road I had planned to take. This was not supposed to be happening . . . but it was.

My life reminded me of the story about a woman who wanted to go on a trip to Italy. She saved her money, learned the language, and planned every aspect of the trip. Finally the day came when she was on the plane headed for Italy. But when the plane landed she heard the flight attendant announce, "Welcome to Holland." She pressed her call button and told the flight attendant that there had to be a mistake. She was supposed to be in Italy. The flight attendant explained, "This plane does not go to Italy." The woman immediately asked when the next plane to Italy would leave, only to have the attendant reply, "I'm sorry, but there are no planes to Italy."

At that moment the woman realized she had two choices. She could spend the rest of her life angry, bitter, and disappointed, or she could embrace Holland and all its beauty. Jim and I chose to embrace Shelly and help her become all that was possible for her.

Where are we now? Shelly has graduated from high school, is driving her own car, and has a job. She's a gold-medal swimmer with the Special Olympics, sings in our church choir, and has been on two mission trips to Honduras and Jamaica. Shelly's life is full of love—a love she shares with everyone she meets. We are all more like Christ because she is part of our lives.

As it turned out, Holland is a beautiful place and, these days, I very rarely think of Italy.

—Anne C. Pierson

What joy upon the honoured sire must come
When showing forth the wisdom of his child!
Lo, she is fair and pure and undefiled—
Thanks, thanks to her, the gladness of his home!

— Rahel Morpurgo

All children are artists, and it is an indictment of our culture that so many of them lose their creativity, their unfettered imaginations, as they grow older.

— Madeleine L'Engle

June 11, 1995

*Y*ou and I went to the mall after church. You slipped your hand in mine as we walked from store to store. Oh! The sweetness! I know that soon you'll have completed turning the corner into young womanhood . . . and you won't do that anymore . . . Oh how sweet it is to savor it now, while you still do!

—Paula Y. Flautt, Journal for My Daughters

Wild West City

*W*e were standing in a canyon, a stone slash in the earth. With the morning sun oozing through the old-growth forest . . . I could actually feel the vulgarities of shopping-mall America falling away . . . I felt linked to the great American nature lovers—to Emerson and John Muir—to every plain, noble man who had ever drawn strength at the breast of Mother Earth. Gazing down at the river, I reached down and stroked Rebecca's hair. . . .

"Hey, Dad," Josh whined. "How much longer do we have to hike?"

Our vacation compromise with the kids had been simple. In the mornings, we had agreed, we would do what Mom and Dad wanted to do, that is, go on inspirational family hikes through the national forest. And in the afternoons we would do what the kids wanted to do, that is, go to some dumb, overcrowded, money-sucking theme park / water park / sideshow tourist attraction. . . .

Like all fathers, I have spent a good chunk of my time in Roadside Attraction America. From Walt Disney World, the apex of kid capitalism, to Uncle Franklin's Petting Zoo and Jam Stand, which featured four ducks, a mangy dog, and two jars of peach preserves, I have followed my kids into hundreds of aquariums, theme parks and pinball / video emporiums. . . .

But of all the stops on the kid carnival circuit, Wild West City turned out to be both the most pathetic and the most profound.

The gimmick was the Wild West in fifteen acres. Wooden sidewalks, buckboards, livery stable, sheriff's office, dry goods store, outlaws, posses, the whole shootin' match. It didn't exactly work.

We paid a king's ransom to a middle aged woman dressed like an old codger and walked through the entrance shed out onto Main Street. It looked like the set of a PTA production of Oklahoma. . . .

There was a bank robbery scheduled for three o' clock in the town square. Right on cue, a desperado came racing out of the bank carrying a sack of money. Two problems: first, he didn't look much like Jesse James. He was wearing a tank top and a Mighty Ducks ball cap. And second, he didn't leap onto a horse to make a getaway. He just ran around the corner and ducked into the employees' lounge. . . .

We tried the Old West bumper boats . . . the engine exhaust gathered into a noxious blue cloud that gave me a headache. . . .

Over at the Old West mule ride, the kid in charge, who had a plastic handlebar mustache clipped into his nostrils . . . helped Rebecca get on the mule without so much as a "Howdy." Then he turned the mule's head toward its tail, spinning the animal in a slow circle . . . the ride lasted four seconds.

The most interesting thing about Wild West City was that the kids just plain loved it. This was the dreariest place I had ever been. . . . But the kids just didn't notice how bad this place was. . . . As evening came, Jody and I sat, exhausted. . . . We both felt we had entered the Twilight Zone. We just watched the kids caper around. And then . . . I swear I suddenly began to feel the same sense of tranquility I had felt that morning. . . .

The children had a burble all of their own. They were as urgent and wild and unsullied as any forest. Unlike Mom and Dad, they don't need beauty to feel sublime. They can feel holy anywhere. As the noise and confusion of modern America faded away as surely as it had that morning in the forest, I could feel my pulse . . . beating to the elemental rhythm of youth.

—Hugh O'Neill, *A Man Called Daddy*

*O*ur greatest obligation to our children is to prepare them to understand and to deal effectively with the world in which they will live and not with the world we have known or the world we would prefer to have.

— Grayson Kirk

*B*etween the dark and the daylight,
When the night is beginning to lower,
Comes a pause in the day's occupations,
That is known as the Children's Hour.

— Henry Wadsworth Longfellow

May 4, 1996

 *I*n the last few months you have transformed! You're almost as tall as me . . . wear my shoe size . . . not a little girl anymore (though parts of your heart will always be!) Suddenly I turn around, and you're turning the corner . . . it begins.

—Paula Y. Flautt, Journal for My Daughters

Thou, straggler into loving arms,
Young climber up of knees,
When I forget thy thousand ways,
Then life and all shall cease.

— Mary Lamb

Standing, with reluctant feet,
Where the brook and river meet,
Womanhood and childhood fleet!

— Henry Wadsworth Longfellow

*B*lessed by childhood, which brings down something of heaven into the midst of our rough earthliness.

— Henri Frederic Amiel

*T*he finest inheritance you can give to a child is to allow it to make its own way, completely on its own feet.

— Isadora Duncan

Going Steady

She hadn't been sixteen very long when she announced to the family that she was going steady. Well, she told her mother and the rest of us found out. She had been dating this guy for a little while but now it was official. She had the class ring with all the tape to prove it.

What a fine romance!

Leigh was happy because she had a boyfriend. Peg was happy because he was a courteous, fine-looking boy with good manners, who spent part of each visit to our house showering his attention on Leigh's mother.

And I was happy, too, because he lived fifty miles away and could only come to see Leigh once a week. Phone calls were long distance, so even they were few and short. What a fine romance. It was all a dad could hope for if his only daughter insisted on having a boyfriend.

She was happy. He was happy. Peg was happy and I was happy. Everybody was happy. Everybody except one football player who had been in school with Leigh since they were in fifth grade.

He had been there the first day she had worn braces to school. He had been there many, many months later when they were gone and she had a set of lovely, straight teeth behind her smile. He had been there the first morning she had worn her glasses and also the day she had put them aside for contacts. He had watched as her mother finally gave up on the short, easy-to-fix hairdo and as Leigh's face was framed by long tresses that spilled over her shoulders. For some reason, he was not happy.

"What a waste, Leigh. You are just too young to go steady," said the football player. "It's all right to date that old boy once a week, but there are six other nights. To sit home all week, what a waste. You are just too young to go steady."

Sooner or later Leigh and the tall, dark, largely absent boyfriend did decide to stop going steady and be "just friends." As soon as the football player heard this news, he asked her for a date. On the first date he asked her to go out the next night. On the second night he said to her, "Will you go steady with me?"

"No," she replied.

"Be my steady girlfriend," he urged.

"I can't be yours. I just got myself back."

— Bob Benson

$\mathscr{B}$ehold, children are a heritage from the Lord, the fruit of the womb is a reward.

— Psalm 127:3

$\mathscr{T}$hat's what being young is all about. You have the courage and the daring to think that you can make a difference. You're not prone to measure your energies in time. You're not likely to live by equations.

— Ruby Dee

December, 1996

  Christmas marked a major point in my life. I have always created the wonder and fun of Christmas for the family . . . mothers do that. But this year you became a co-creator with me! One day I came home and found you'd spent the afternoon making elaborate paper snowflakes from the Martha Stewart magazine . . . Christmas Eve you laboriously peeled oranges to make curls . . . peeled and chopped ginger, made a syrup, and mixed a punch.

—Paula Y. Flautt, Journal for My Daughters

*N*othing you do for children is ever wasted. They seem not to notice us, hovering, averting our eyes, and they seldom offer thanks, but what we do for them is never wasted.

— Garrison Keillor

*N*ature fits all her children with something to do.

— James Russell Lowell

*Y*ou bring them into the world saying good-bye.

—Anonymous

There is no more beautiful witness to the mystery of the word made flesh than a baby's naked body. I remember with sensory clarity sitting with one of my babies on my lap and running my hand over the incredibly pure smoothness of the bare back and thinking that any mother, holding her child thus, must have at least an echo of what it is like to be Mary; that in touching the particular created matter, flesh, of our child, we are touching the Incarnation.

— Madeleine L'Engle

$\mathscr{A}$ child's attitude toward everything is an artist's attitude.

—Willa Cather

$\mathscr{W}$hen my three children were talking about getting married, one thing I told each of them to remember was, "If there's something about your prospective spouse that you can't stand now, multiply that one thousand times, and that's how bad it's going to feel after you are married . . . So be careful about choosing a spouse. If God didn't put you together, don't you get together.

—Thelma Wells

*W*ithin thirty seconds of my entering the door, both of my knees are attacked by two squealing girls. A fuzzy-headed infant is placed in my arms. . . .

"The cavalry is here," I announce.

"And none too soon," my wife . . . replies with a grateful smile.

The next few hours bring a chorus of family noises. . . . The conversation is as continuous as it is predictable.

"Jenna has my doll!"

"Can I hold the baby?"

"Honey, where is the pacifier?" . . .

"Girls, it's time to go to bed."

"One more song?"

— Max Lucado

How pleasant it is for a father to sit at his child's board. It is like an aged man reclining under the shadow of an oak which he has planted.

— Sir Walter Scott

Grown-ups never understand anything for themselves, and it is tiresome for children to be always and forever explaining things to them.

— Antoine de Saint-Exupery

January, 1997

*Y*ou see things differently. . . . We were driving downtown to the convention center. I was saying "Hurray!" because I'd made it. About that time I missed the entrance to the parking garage and was bemoaning having to drive around the block. "It's okay," you proclaim. "You're taking a victory lap!"

—Paula Y. Flautt, Journal for My Daughters

The thoughts of a daughter are a kind memorial.

— Enid Bagnold

What music is more enchanting than the voices of young people, when you can't hear what they say?

— Logan Pearsall Smith

Flowers and children—emblems meet,
Of all things innocent and sweet.

— Marguerite Blessington

What are little girls made of?
Sugar and spice, and everything nice;
That's what little girls are made of.

— Anonymous

When I was a kid and an argument broke out in our home, my dad always used to say, "We may have a few differences inside these walls, but you remember, we're family. If your brother or your sister needs you, you take care of 'em. You love 'em. You pull for 'em."

— Charles R. Swindoll

July 20, 1996

  *T*his summer there's been such growth in acknowledging mistakes and forgiving others. What answered prayers! Last evening you and Grandma and Curry and I were playing cards—You and Curry got into it, and she hit you. After a bit she was sorry, but you weren't interested. Later, drifting off to sleep, you said, " Tell Curry I forgive her."

—Paula Y. Flautt, Journal for My Daughters

My Child, My Friend

$\mathcal{F}$rom the moment I first held you in my arms, still drenched in birth, until now as I watch you drive away to the appointments you've made with life, mothering you has been my life's most awesome, fearsome, and joyful adventure. I didn't know that first day what mothering really meant, though I was eager to begin. You seemed so fragile then, so small and trusting—depending on me for every life-sustaining need. I thought at first you'd break.

"Be sure to support the little head," they told me. But I was soon to learn that you were tougher than you looked and could out-squeal, out-sleep, and out-endure me, ten to one. In fact, those first three months, I wondered if I'd ever finish a meal or a night's sleep again.

The teaching began immediately. I had studied to be a teacher, but it seemed to me that there was never a classroom student as hungry to learn as you. Before you could speak, your eyes asked the questions and your tiny hands reached to touch and learn, taste and see. It wasn't long, though, until your cooing turned inquisitive, every babbled sentence ending with a question mark. Your first words were: "What's that? What's that?" Soon your questing vocabulary grew, and you were begging, "Teach me something, Mommy. Teach me something."

I would stop to teach you: numbers and names of things—textures, shapes, sizes, foods, furniture, pets, trees, flowers, stars, and clouds. Soon you were teaching me. Teaching me that when the lesson stopped, learning kept going.

You taught me to see the miracles I'd stumbled over every day. You taught me trust and delight and ecstasy. You held a mirror up before my attitudes and role-played all my reactions. You taught me what it meant to live what I verbalized, to believe what I preached, to internalize what I lectured.

You, who came to me all wet from birth, baptized the common things with natal freshness and with the shower of your laughter, washed away the barnacles of grown-up cynicism and the dust of dull routine. You made things new. You gave me an excuse to be myself again, to skip down forest trails or sled the frozen hillsides, clean with snow, to splash through springtime puddles—barefoot-glad—and guess at where the shooting stars must go.

You gave me eyes to see the realness of people once again, to look beyond their faces' thin facades. You saw the child inside the aged, the longing and the passion entrapped by gnarled joints and failing eyesight. You recognized profundity and wisdom in the giggly, teenage baby-sitter, beauty in the plain, and creativity in the timid. You showed me that the generation gap is an artificial invention of our culture and bigotry a perversion of nature's celebration of variety.

I have helped you learn to crawl, toddle, walk, run, swim, dance, ride bikes, and drive the car. I have encouraged you to stand tall, walk alone, run from evil, dance for joy, ride out the hard times, and drive yourself on when you felt tempted to give up. I have been there waiting when you crossed the road, climbed off the school bus, came in from dates, and returned home from college. Now, about all I can do for you is be there, because gradually you have come to be your own person— not so much my child as my friend.

— Gloria Gaither

*A*las! I let you leave me, my child, you, the light of my eyes.

—Tobit 10:5

I got more children than I can rightly take care of, but I ain't got more than I can love.

— Ossie Guffy

*T*hese are my daughters, I suppose. But where in the world did the children vanish?

— Phyllis McGinley

September 19, 1987

$\mathcal{I}$t was] the day before you're fifth birthday. You figured out that if Anna's swing was tied to yours you could swing her too when you pumped. So, you went and found a strap and hooked them together. It worked beautifully! I glanced out the window and saw curls swaying in the sunshine and heard giggles in the air.

—Paula Y. Flautt, Journal for My Daughters

Whenever I feel myself inferior to everything about me, threatened by my own mediocrity, frightened by the discovery that a muscle is losing its strength, a desire its power, or a pin the keen edge of its bite, I can still hold up my head and say to myself: . . . "Let me not forget that I am the daughter of a woman who bent her head, trembling, between the blades of a cactus, her wrinkled face full of ecstasy over the promise of a flower, a woman who herself never ceased to flower, untiringly, during three quarters of a century."

— Colette

Labored Joy

World War II was barely over when I got the telegram. My wife of thirteen years wired me urgently in Guam—she had just learned that she was expecting our first child! We had been told time and again that we could not conceive children, and the news was nothing short of a miracle.

But I was on a tour of duty that wouldn't end before the baby's birth. And if there was any place in the world I wanted to be, it was at the U.S. Navy Hospital in San Diego that coming September. There wasn't much I could say to my commanding officer—there were guys with sick parents, guys with broken hearts, guys with bigger problems than mine who wanted to get home. I had men under my command who were pleading with me for furlough. The one thing I knew I could do was pray. And that's what I did.

One night, aboard ship, the desire to get home to my wife lay heavy on my heart. I was on night watch, and as the hours ticked by, I paced the deck, talking to God. I was pretty much by myself, and toward the end of the watch I knelt in prayer. As I prayed, the anxiety and discontentment I had felt since my wife's telegram began to fade. Instead, I felt a sense of peace and joy. Though I dearly wanted to be with my wife during this precious time, somehow I felt content and I was sure that my prayers had been heard.

Forty-eight hours later, I heard my name at mail call, I recognized at once that the letter for me was from the naval base in San Diego. With no word of explanation, I was ordered home. And it looked like, if all went smoothly, that I would be there in early September.

It was a typical case of "hurry up and wait." By the time all the connections were made, I was at my wife's side only one day before she went into labor. She was thirty-five years old, and the labor was long and hard. The day passed, and the night, and still she labored. In those days, fathers weren't allowed in the delivery room, so I paced the streets drinking chocolate malts, one after another, praying for a safe birth.

At six o' clock the following morning, the doctor appeared in the waiting room. "It's a girl!" he said, "And she's healthy and strong."

I quickly made my way to the viewing window and looked at the babies, all lined up in a row. I knew my daughter immediately. She looked like me, and her mother, and my father, and a lot of other relatives, all rolled into one. She was beautiful.

When we finally took her home, I walked the floor with her, singing in my off-key voice about far-away places with strange sounding names. I bought her a music box that played "Anchors Aweigh." I told her stories about ships, and sailors and seas and tides, and I told her about an answered prayer that brought me home from sea to be with my little girl.

— G. J., San Diego, Calif., (from *Butterfly Kisses & Bittersweet Tears* by Bob Carlisle)

$\mathcal{I}$t is a rare privilege to watch the birth, growth, and first feeble struggles of a living mind.

— Annie Sullivan

$\mathcal{H}$ope of my life! Dear children of my heart!
That anxious heart, to each fold feeling true,
To you still pants each pleasure to impart.

— Georgiana Cavendish

Good Roots, Strong Love

*W*as I the one who secretly doubted that one little baby could significantly change our lives? . . . I had a lot to learn! We are indeed very different with you! The days that were ours have all become yours.

Did I often make it hard for you, those first months? There I was trying to soothe you with one arm, furiously turning the pages of my Dr. Spock with the other. I really apologize for being so new and shaky! . . . It seems so much better now. I mean, I'm far from a pro, but I do think I'm getting used to us. . . .

Your daddy wrote a poem about us which says that we three are like a strong tree with good roots. One of us alone would be buffeted by the wind. But together we're strong.

You two nourish me with your love.

— Paula D'Arcy (from *The Gift of a Child*
by Marion Stroud)

February 28, 1996

This afternoon there were things to do. Important things. But Curry, having read an article on botanical pressing and drying, was busy pressing spider mums pulled out of the arrangement on the dining room table. . . . Anna having discovered an old piano book of mine was engrossed with learning Beethoven's *Moonlight Sonata*. . . . Surely there are times when the thing to do, the most important thing, is the chance to move in chosen pursuits of who you are becoming.

—Paula Y. Flautt, Journal for My Daughters

A Kiss in the Dark

Daddy."

The voice was coming from another world—the world of the awake. I ignored it and stayed in the world of slumber.

"Daddy." The voice was insistent.

I opened one eye. Andrea, our three-year-old, was at the edge of my bed only inches from my face.

"Daddy, I'm scared."

I opened the other eye. It was three in the morning.

"What's wrong?"

"I need a fwashwight in my woom."

"What?"

"I need a fwashwight in my woom."

"Why?"

" 'Cause it's dark."

I told her the lights were on. I told her the night-light was on and the hall light was on.

"But Daddy," she objected, "what if I open my eyes and can't see anything?" . . .

My wife interrupted . . . there was a power failure around midnight . . . Andrea must have awakened in the dark. . . .

Even the hardest of hearts would be touched by the thought of a child walking up in darkness so black she couldn't find her way out of her room.

I climbed out of bed, picked Andrea up, got a flashlight . . . and carried her to bed. All the while, I told her that Mom and Dad were here and that she didn't need to be afraid. I tucked her in and gave her a kiss.

And that was enough for Andrea.

— Max Lucado

If I can stop one heart from breaking

I shall not live in vain.

If I can ease one life from aching , or cool one pain,

Or help one fainting robin into this nest again,

I shall not live in vain.

—Emily Dickinson

There are only two lasting bequests we can hope to give our children. One of these is roots, the other is wings.

— Holding Carter

Daughter am I in my mother's house;
But mistress in my own.

— Rudyard Kipling

For a good-natured girl is loved best in the main,
If her dress is but decent, though ever so plain.

— Ann Taylor

May 7, 1998

*Y*ou just finished opening night of *Alice in Wonderland* as a Dream Creature. You filled the stage with mime, dance, and character! And now, after showering all the glitter out of your hair, you're sitting up in bed munching gouda cheese and reading books from years ago—a box of them, drug from a closet, sits by your bed: *The Little Engine That Could, The Little Penguin, Pepper* (from my childhood!) . . . How dear this is to me! Almost sixteen, yet words and memories from childhood still resonate . . . meaningful connections to the heart.

—Paula Y. Flautt, Journal for My Daughters

Laughter: A Gracious Gift

As I rocked Shaohannah to sleep tonight, I once again had a thousand thoughts cross my mind about the miracle that happened in our family on March 15, 2000. Six of us—my husband Steven, myself, our three biological children, and a dear friend—headed to China on March 11, 2000. We returned on March 22, 2000. We left Tennessee missing something, but returned from China complete.

Shaohannah (pronounced "Show-Hannah") Hope Yan Chapman (we call her Shaoey for short) entered our arms on the nineteenth floor of the Grand Sun City Hotel in Changsha, China, on March 15, 2000. It is something supernatural that happens. We were an instant family.

It has been almost six months since we returned with our bundle of Hunan energy, and a day never passes that we can't believe how blessed we are by this precious treasure that has been entrusted to our care. We have all been so impacted by this little girl that God placed in our family. Shaohannah, who is all of 29 ⅕ inches long and 19 pounds 3 ounces, is the center of attention at our house these days. Our oldest daughter, Emily (age fourteen), absolutely loves and adores her. She spends most of her free time with her little sister and when we need it, she is a world-class babysitter!

Our boys, Caleb (age eleven) and Will Franklin (age nine), are definitely going to be better dads and husbands because of their beautiful little sister. Changing diapers and clothes, packing diaper bags, loading strollers in cars, and keeping Shaoey entertained in her car seat are all tasks that they are becoming very proficient at! They are absolutely in love with her and would do anything for her. It is a privilege to watch all of the children growing up together.

The abundance of laughter in our home today is worth all the paper-work we went through to adopt Shaoey (in Chinese Shao, spelled Xiao, means "laughter"). We continue to be grateful for a birth mom and dad who gave the gift of life to our little girl, whom we are so privileged to love, cherish, and raise. . . . Our hope is that someday we will return and show our daughter where she came from so that she will know how special her homeland and people are.

Shaohannah is a gift of God's miraculous grace (Hannah means "gift of God's grace") to our family. . . . We are so blessed.

— Mary Beth Chapman

August 9, 1997

$\mathcal{I}$ wasn't feeling well today. You brought me tea in a pink china cup—chamomile. "It's soothing," you said. On the saucer lay a sprig of pink yarrow you'd picked in the garden. Always you bless with a gentle touch—tender, thoughtful touch, and a touch of beauty—my darling girl!

—Paula Y. Flautt, Journal for My Daughter

*J*ust let me play in my room all by myself! But could you
stay up here and work? I want to be by myself, but Mommy,
make warm noises I can hear.

— Gloria Gaither

*T*wo good little children, named Mary and Ann,
Both haply live, as good girls always can,
And though they are not either sullen or mute,
They seldom or never are heard to dispute.

—Ann Taylor

Laughter in the Walls

I pass a lot of houses on my way home—
Some pretty,
Some expensive,
Some inviting—
But my heart always skips a beat
When I turn down the road
And see my house nestled against the hill.

I guess I'm especially proud
Of the house and the way it looks because
I drew the plans myself.

It started out large enough for us—
I even had a study—
Two teenaged boys now reside in there.
And it had a guest room—
My girl and nine dolls are permanent guests.
It had a small room that Peg
Had hoped would be her sewing room—
Two boys swinging on the dutch door
Have claimed this room as their own.

So it really doesn't look right now
As if I'm much of an architect.
But it will get larger again—
One by one they will go away

To work,
To college,
To service,
To their own houses,
And then there will be room—
A guest room,
A study,
And a sewing room
For just the two of us.
But it won't be empty—
Every corner
Every room

Every nick
In the coffee table
Will be crowded with memories.
Memories of picnics,
Parties, Christmases,
Bedside vigils, summers,
Fires, winters, going barefoot,
Leaving for vacation, cats.
Conversations, black eyes,
Graduations, first dates,
Ball games, arguments,
Washing dishes, bicycles,

Dogs, boat rides,
Getting home from vacation,
Meals, rabbits, and
A thousand other things
That fill the lives of those who would raise five.
And Peg and I will sit
Quietly by the fire
And listen to the
Laughter in the walls.

— Bob Benson

$\mathcal{I}$'ve looked on thee as thou wert calmly sleeping,
And wished—oh, couldst thou ever be as blest
As now, when haply all thy cause of weeping
Is for a truant bird or faded rose!

— Katharine Augusta Ware

$\mathcal{T}$here is always one moment in childhood when the door opens and lets the future in.

— Graham Greene

You're Sarah! . . . First we're laughing, then we're crying. We can't believe it. . . . The end was so fast—you insistent, me scared. And your daddy tripping to get into his delivery room 'whites.' And then you. Ten fingers, ten toes, little you. Perfect you.

Watching you stretch your way into this world was the fullest joy I've ever known. Complete. No happiness in my life has ever been that true. I'll carry your first cry with me everywhere I go.

— Paula D'Arcy (from *The Gift of A Child* by Marion Stroud)

September 20, 2000

*E*ighteen! The morning started—as always—with breakfast in bed, flowers, cinnamon rolls, fruit smoothies, birthday cards, and presents for you and Daddy. I watched it all, realizing that this was the last time it would ever be like this. "We're living the butternut speech (from Our Town)," I say. You say, "Oh, Mom." You think I'm always saying "this is the last," "this is almost over." . . . I need to tell you I'm not being depressed or overly dramatic. I'm realizing and seeing and valuing . . . but of course your view is different from mine . . . angled by a different age, a different season.

—Paula Y. Flautt, Journal for My Daughters

𝓡ock-a bye baby in the treetops
When the wind blows the cradle will rock . . .

—Traditional

𝓦hen the voices of children are heard on the green
And laughing is heard on the hill,
My heart is at rest within my breast
And everything else is still.

—William Blake

Good News and Bad News

"How was your day at school?" I asked as you sat in the tub soaking off the day's collection of grime and odors.

"Okay, I guess."

"Oh, c'mon. What happened?"

"Well, good things and bad. You know I told you I couldn't seem to get everyone to be friends at the same time? Well, Sally and Susan both like me okay, but they wouldn't play with each other. But today I got them to make up and be friends."

"That's great don't you think?"

"Well, yes, but they both got to playing together so well that they left me out and I was alone the rest of the day."

"Oh . . ."

I waited in silence, and you shrugged your little boney, soapy shoulders and looked at me timidly.

"Oh, well, blessed are the peacemakers."

Then you managed a crooked little grin that made me know that today was being chalked up to your store of wisdom, and that the growing you had done would somehow make tomorrow a little bit richer for it.

— Gloria Gaither

January 15, 2001

Where are you headed in this life? As a little girl you'd wander through home stores picking up carpet samples, fabric swatches, color chips; you'd think up myriad business ideas, setting up a lemonade stand, being the top seller of festival tickets for your school. You said you wanted to build a building and take care of people. [At] a production of Shakespear's *Twelfth Night,* you leaned over and whispered, "I want to be either a doctor or a teacher."

Hmmm . . . designing, selling, performing, healing, teaching . . . I am trusting . . .

—Paula Y. Flautt, Journal for My Daughters

The Old Guitar

When I was a young man, I used to play the guitar and sing, and people were kind enough to tell me that I was rather good at it. I played at church functions, and occasionally for a wedding or family event. As a child, my little daughter always seemed proud of my amateur performances.

But as the years went by, life got busier and busier, and the old guitar collected a lot of dust. I rarely got it out and played it, and when I did, I was always surprised at how rusty my fingers were and how terrible my voice sounded to me. The less I played and sang, the more self-conscious I became.

My daughter grew up and got married, and now she has a son of her own. One night, when she and her little boy were staying at our house, she went into the room where he slept to tell him goodnight. As

I walked by, I heard her singing a song that I'd played for her when she was a child. Impulsively, I went into the den and found the old guitar. I wiped it off with a cloth and joined the two of them. And we began to sing.

Before the night had passed, I think we must have gone through every song I'd ever learned. We harmonized, tried to remember long-lost words, and reminisced until nearly midnight. My grandson finally fell asleep, but before he did he said, "Grandpa, you have a good voice. I didn't know you could sing."

I smiled at him, kissed him, and congratulated myself on not sounding so bad after all. And, unwilling to let the magic end, while he dozed, my daughter and I sang one more song together before we said goodnight.

— T. W., Summerville, S.C. (from *Butterfly Kisses & Bittersweet Tears* by Bob Carlisle)

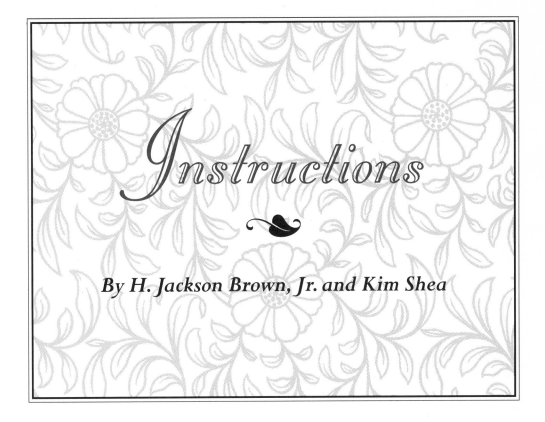

Instructions

By H. Jackson Brown, Jr. and Kim Shea

Life's Little Instruction Book, the [#]1 *New York Times* bestseller that has been translated into more than thirty languages, was begun as loving advice from a father to a son—H. Jackson Brown, Jr. to his son, Adam. Several years later it became the inspiration for some heartfelt words of advice that Kim Shea wrote for her daughters, Cassaday Ann, Kennedy Jo, Clarity Grace, and Century Eva. The two parents began sharing and comparing their insights and eventually collaborated on *Life's Little Instruction Book from Mothers to Daughters,* (ISBN: 1-55853-832-1), a collection of nearly 500 bits and sound advice and thoughtful reminders for creating a happy life and loving home. They have selected some of their favorite entries for this special collection. To enjoy them all, pick up a copy of the complete book.

1 · Be the person you'd be proud of your daughter becoming.

2 · Form good habits. They are as hard to break as bad ones.

3 · Never do anything that would cause you to lose the trust and affection of your husband and children.

4 · Remember the three essentials of a happy household: prayer, patience and praises.

5 · Devote time to your child's scrapbook. Today's special moments are tomorrow's treasured memories.

6 · Give more gifts than you receive.

7 · When you want to be taken seriously, dress seriously.

8 · Life is a dance. Don't sit it out.

9 · Never order French onion soup on a first date.

10 · Remember that some things are urgent, and others are important. Know the difference.

11 · Praise your children's good decisions and good choices, not their good luck.

12 · Remember that all happy marriages are the result of compromising and forgiving.

13 · Sit down in new clothes before cutting off the tags.

14 · When your heart has been broken, put yourself in a situation where it can get broken again. It's the best cure.

15 · Identify those things that make you the happiest. Allow yourself time to do them.

16 · Surround yourself with people who support your virtues, not ones who test your vices.

17 · When traveling, never pack a linen suit.

18 · Always paint your toenails red when wearing a new pair of sandals.

19 · Know how to make a campfire and change a tire.

20 · Kiss your husband passionately in an unexpected moment.

21 · Be the aunt whom all of your nieces and nephews refer to as their favorite.

22 · Always look the person in the eyes when saying, "I'm sorry."

23 · Always look the person in the eyes when saying, "I forgive you."

24 · Always look the person in the eyes when saying, "I love you."

25 · Remember that nothing is a bargain if you don't need it.

26 · When searching for the love of your life, remember that you might have to date a lot of lemons before you find the peach.

27 · Place a high value on the friends who help you move.

28 · Never stop sharpening your computer skills.

29 · Remember that wealth and wisdom mean little unless shared.

30 · Don't be in such a hurry pursuing your dreams that you rush right past them.

31 · Never refuse to answer another question from your inquisitive youngster, no matter how tempting it may be.

32 · Never speak negatively about one friend to another friend.

33 · Surround your workspace with pictures drawn by your children.

34 · Never forget that being loved is better
than being rich.

35 · If you're trying to decide if someone's
action warrants a thank-you note, the
answer is always yes.

36 · Savor the words "I love you" each and
every time you hear them.

37 · Feed a calf with a bottle.

38 · Keep extra gifts on hand for spur-of-the-moment events.

39 · If someone plans a good surprise for you, act surprised.

40 · Never stay more than twenty minutes
when visiting a non-family member in the
hospital.

41 · Never keep anything from your doctor.

42 · Never start a diet on a weekend.

43 · Never make an important decision when you're upset or angry.

44 · Never get serious with a man who has more shoes than you do.

45 · If you're wondering what to do with your afternoon, visit a library or a bookstore.

46 · View the ring in the bathtub as evidence
that your children had a good day.

47 · Be faithful to your husband, your heart,
and your hairdresser.

48 · Dive for the bouquet.

49 · Determine your response to temptation long before it taps you on the shoulder.

50 · Hold a newborn baby any time you get the chance.

51 · Add an extra egg and a teaspoon of vanilla to a cake mix to make it taste more like homemade.

52 · Every once in a while, let your boss see you sweat.

53 · Be the person your friends refer to as their best friend.

54 · To keep from misplacing your keys or purse, put them in the same place every time you enter your house.

55 · Never pass up an opportunity to hold your dad's hand, regardless of your age.

56 · Don't be afraid occasionally to rock the boat.

57 · Remember that when you grow old with the one you love, your love will never grow old.

58 · Don't consider buying a bigger water heater as an extravagance. You never ever want to run out of hot water.

59 · Pray for our leaders.

60 · Never let your gas gauge drop below a quarter tank.

61 · Keep a $20 bill hidden in your car for emergencies.

62 · When you've decided to give up on something or someone, give it just one more try.

63 · Do more than expected and no one will ever be disappointed in you.

64 · Keep several postage stamps in your billfold.

65 · Label and file your photographs in a photo album as soon as you bring them home.

66 · Be the reason someone becomes inspired today.

67 · If you go to the movies with someone you want to be close to, leave your sweater at home.

68 · Never miss your annual physical.

69 · Eat lots of warm oatmeal. Don't forget the brown sugar and raisins.

70 · Remember that a smile is the quickest way to improve your appearance.

71 · Measure your success as a parent not by what your children are accomplishing, but by the kind of people they are becoming.

72 · Count blessings, not calories.

73 · Think twice before saying "yes" to a stranger.

74 · Think twice before saying "no" to a friend.

75 · Drink your morning coffee from the most interesting, brightly colored mug you can find.

76 · Become a favorite customer at your favorite stores.

77 · Consider giving trees as gifts; they're perfect for weddings, showers, new babies, housewarmings, and retirements.

78 · Never miss an opportunity to tell someone you love them.

79 · Own a world globe, a good dictionary, and a good thesaurus. Refer to them often.

80 · Remember that every backyard needs a swing.

81 · Say something positive as early as possible every day.

82 · Don't go overboard when planning your wedding. The thousands of dollars and hundreds of hours spent by brides and their mothers trying to create the perfect wedding has never guaranteed a lasting, happy marriage.

83 · Listen carefully when the people who know you best say something is a bad idea.

84 • Wade in a creek every chance you get.

85 • Always take your vacation days.

86 • Always compliment the cook.

87 • Never go to bed with dishes in the sink.

88 • Never miss an opportunity to ride a roller coaster.

89 • Clean out your purse at least once a month.

90 • Never go on a date without cab fare home and coins for a phone call.

91 · Remember that everyone you meet is
hungry for a kind word.

92 · To get the job you want, excel at the job
you have.

93 · Remember that it's important to be your
children's friend, but more important to
be their mother.

94 · When buying clothes, shoes, or jewelry, remember that if it's cheap, it probably looks it.

95 · Be known for your warm embrace, your thoughtful heart, and your generous spirit.

96 · Make homemade peach ice cream.

97 · Make new friends but treasure the old.

98 · Don't forget that men like to receive flowers too.

99 · Be the person your friends call when they need advice, ideas, or help.

100 · Make visiting your elderly loved ones a
priority.

101 · Never marry for money. You'll pay too
much.

102 · Turn off the television. Pull out the
Scrabble game.

103 · Never argue over the position of the toilet seat. It's not that important.

104 · Never work for a person you wouldn't be proud to introduce to your mother.

105 · Encourage people to like you by liking them first.

106 · Save some of the money you make.

107 · Keep all the promises you make.

108 · Share the movement of your unborn child with your husband at every opportunity. There is no feeling more precious or joy more complete.

109 · Learn to bake homemade bread.

110 · Run away for the weekend. Take your husband. Leave the children.

111 · Keep housework in perspective. Your children will remember how happy their
home was, not how spotless.

112 · Never reveal personal information during a telephone call that you didn't initiate.

113 · Let your best friend hear you refer to her as your best friend.

114 · Remember that people forget what you say, and what you do, but they never forget the way you make them feel.

115 • Send a thank-you note to your boss after receiving any raise or performance award.

116 • Be nice to your sisters. They may turn out to be your best friends.

117 • Live within your means even if it means living without your wants.

118 · Work in a political campaign for a candidate you admire.

119 · When nothing is going well, call your grandmother.

120 · Use the phrase "I need your help" with your children often. Whether you actually need their help in all cases is unimportant.

121 · Don't rush to bail your children out of trouble for which they are responsible.

122 · Never forget that it's more important to be beautiful to listen to than to be beautiful to look at.

123 · Overpay good baby-sitters.

124 · Never regret any money spent on books or flowers.

125 · Never run out of peanut butter.

126 · Few things are as important as they first seem. Ask yourself, "Will this make a difference in my life a year from now?"

127 · Talk about your family history often.
Always be proud of your heritage.

128 · Be selective with your bumper stickers. The
novelty wears off, but the glue rarely does.

129 · Be the one who always remembers to
bring a camera and extra film.

130 · Remember that the important thing is not what you have in your life, but whom.

131 · Never buy a bridesmaid's dress thinking you'll ever wear it again.

132 · Own something perfect to wear if the employer or date of your dreams requests to see you today.

133 · Recall your favorite childhood memories,
then recreate them for your children.

134 · Master the art of making a beautiful
sandwich.

135 · Don't trust skinny Italian chefs.

136 · When you see an extraordinarily beautiful
sunset, take a few moments to enjoy it.

137 · Keep a family Bible on the coffee table.
Leave the pages open to your favorite
verse.

138 · Never interrupt a person telling a joke by
saying, "Oh, I've heard it before."

139 · When you're angry at your husband, remember that he's the only person your children love as much as they love you.

140 · Keep your priorities straight. If you are too busy to do a favor for a friend, you're too busy.

141 · Share most of the cookies you make.

142 · Write down immediately all those cute things that your children say.

143 · Never give a gift that requires batteries without including the batteries.

144 · Remember that everyone you meet wants to be noticed, to be heard, to be appreciated, and to be loved.

145 · Attack the problem, not the person.

146 · When donating an old purse to charity, slip a five-dollar bill inside to give the new owner a nice little surprise.

147 · Be known for giving the neighborhood's best Halloween treats.

148 · Learn to put your heart on paper. The written word can be much more powerful than the spoken one.

149 · Be proud, but not boastful.

150 · Be confident, but not conceited.

151 · Be strong, but not inflexible.

152 · Be brave, but not reckless.

153 · Remember that character shines, beauty fades.

154 · Call someone you love and tell them so.

155 · Grant yourself incredible freedom by overcoming the need to please all people all of the time.

156 · When you want to know how you really look, ask a five-year-old.

157 · Never buy a swimsuit thinking you will look great in it if you lose a couple of pounds.

158 · Return phone calls the same day that you receive them.

159 · Whenever you're headed out for an appointment that may involve some waiting time, take along a book.

160 · Teach your children to pray. There are no sweeter words than "God bless Mommy and God bless Daddy."

161 · Never give a gift that's not beautifully wrapped.

162 · Compliment your husband and your children every day.

163 · Celebrate with your husband the anniversary of your first date. If possible, spend it the same way you did the first time.

164 · If you have the honor of being in someone's wedding, send them an anniversary card every year.

165 · When traveling, think McDonald's when you need a clean restroom.

166 · Bundle up in a blanket and sit on your front porch on a cold winter's evening.

167 · Remain an optimist. You will always have more fun.

168 · Remember that clean kitchen counters and neatly made-up beds can hide a score of housecleaning shortcomings.

169 · As often as you can, give in to the request for "just one more story, Mommy."

170 · Take time to get to know people. Resist the temptation to judge them by how they look or what they wear.

171 · Don't display hand towels so fancy that your guests are reluctant to use them.

172 · Learn how to make your grandma's special Christmas cookies.

173 · Be guilty of hanging too many Christmas lights.

174 · Remember that socks and underwear don't count as Christmas or birthday presents.

175 · Never allow a friend to cry alone.

176 · When hugging, don't be the first to let go.

177 · Take photographs of the interiors as well as the exteriors of all the places you live, including your dorm rooms. They will recall priceless memories some day.

178 · When disagreements arise, avoid using the words "never" and "always."

179 · Own something made of cashmere that you wear next to your skin.

180 · Wherever you live, always plant a garden, even if it's only basil and rosemary grown in flowerpots on a windowsill.

181 · Resist the temptation to tell all you know.

182 · Be confident enough in your resumé and your bra size that neither needs to be even the slightest bit padded.

183 · Be tactful and considerate when quitting a job or breaking up with a boyfriend. You just might want to be welcomed back one day.

184 · Visit an Amish community. Buy a loaf of bread, and if you can afford it, a handmade quilt. There is no better quality of either available elsewhere.

185 · Avoid gossip.

186 · Never surrender your dreams.

187 · Read the biographies of successful women for inspiration.

188 · Don't automatically trust the biggest ad in the yellow pages.

189 · Own a copy of Louisa May Alcott's *Little Women*. Read it to your daughters.

190 · Never pass up a good garage sale.

191 · Once in your lifetime, discover the romantic appeal of a hayloft.

192 · Remember that successful parenting is based less on what you do for your children and more on what you teach them to do for themselves.

193 · Remember that the best cure for cold
weather is a warm embrace.

194 · Realize that sometimes the best response to
a trying situation is to just grin and bear it.

195 · Be a source of optimism for all who
know you.

196 · Make a list of the ways you and your sister
are alike. Refer to it the next time you are
angry with her.

197 · Remember that happiness depends more
on give than on take.

198 · Slow dance with your husband at every
opportunity.

199 · Remember that children need loving the most when they are the hardest to love.

200 · Never underestimate the power of a little black dress and a strand of real pearls.

201 · Remember, you may be only one person to the world, but you may be the world to one person.

202 • Learn the medical history of women on both sides of your family.

203 • Remember that life's most important events are sometimes disguised as ordinary moments.

204 • Take photographs of your children on their first day of every school year.

205 • Speak positively about others. You will never regret the nice things you say about people.

206 • When living alone, have an unlisted telephone number.

207 • Volunteer to be the banker when playing Monopoly.

208 · Show your children how to clothespin base-
ball cards to the spokes of their bikes to
transform them into roaring motorcycles.

209 · Be more concerned about the direction of
your life than its speed.

210 · When buying a new car or a new dress,
remember you can't lose if you choose red.

211 · Welcome the wondrous feeling of butter-
flies in your stomach that new love brings.

212 · Date many. Fall in love with few. Marry one.

213 · Involve yourself so strongly with a charity
or a cause that people easily associate it
with you.

214 · Remember that throughout life pain is
inevitable but misery is optional.

215 · Teach your children how to lose as well as
how to win.

216 · Remember that life doesn't have to be
perfect to be wonderful.

217 · Have a new college roommate every year. Each one will teach you more about relationships than you can learn anywhere else.

218 · Always kiss your husband on New Year's Eve — even if you have to wake him up.

219 · Own beautifully personalized stationery. Use it often.

220 · Remember that sometimes the nicest thing you can do for yourself is to do something nice for someone else.

221 · Ensure a successful marriage by falling in love over and over with your husband.

222 · Reserve your best behavior for your family, not for strangers.

223 · Remember that while you can't always be right, you can always be courteous.

224 · Find a perfume you love and be loyal to it.

225 · Speak with enthusiasm when describing your husband, children, job, or employer, and give them reasons to do the same when describing you.

226 · Bad things happen in bad places. So stay out of bad places.

227 · When deciding matters of great importance, even after you think you have the answer, give it another twenty-four hours.

228 · When someone offers you a breath mint, take it.

229 · Take care of your reputation. There is nothing that takes a longer time to build or a shorter time to destroy.

230 · Remain just a bit mysterious even to those who think they know everything about you.

231 · Don't waste time trying to make good deals with bad people.

232 · Be an example of what you want to see more of in the world.

233 · Keep a diary of the significant moments in your life.

234 · When scrapes and bruises occur, remember the healing power of a mother's kiss.

235 · Never leave a message on your answering
machine that would indicate that you
might be out of town.

236 · Regardless of the situation, react with class.

237 · Spoil your husband, not your children.

238 · Remember, it's easier to meet the right person after you have become the right person.

239 · Always enjoy a corn dog at the county fair.

240 · Marry the man of your dreams. Never settle for less.

241 · Strive for a peaceful home, not a perfect one.

242 · Never forget how it feels to be sixteen.

243 · I know you will forget this, but try to remember that everything you do as a young girl, teenager, and adult is preparation for you to become the world's greatest mom.

Dreams

Compiled by Paula Y. Flautt

May you live all the days of your life.

— Jonathan Swift

I have a dream that my four little children will one day live
in a nation where they will not be judged by the color of their
skin but by the content of their character.

— Martin Luther King, Jr.

The doors we open and close each day decide the lives we
live.

— Flora Whittemore

There is a life that is worth living now as it was worth living in the former days, and that is the honest life, the useful life, the unselfish life, cleansed by devotion to an ideal. There is a battle worth fighting now as it was worth fighting then, and that is the battle for justice and equality: to make our city and our state free in fact as well as in name; to break the rings that strangle real liberty, and to keep them broken; to cleanse, so far as in our power lies, the fountains of our national life from political, commercial, and social corruption; to teach our sons and daughters, by precept and example, the honor of serving such a country as America. That is work worthy of the finest manhood and womanhood.

— Henry Van Dyke

$\mathcal{N}$o one has ever achieved anything from the smallest to the greatest unless the dream was dreamed first.

— Laura Ingalls Wilder

$\mathcal{E}$very real accomplishment first begins as a dream.

— Alan C. Elliott

$\mathcal{W}$e should see dreaming as one of our responsibilities, rather than an alternative to one.

— Mary Engelbreit

As you discover your purpose in life and pursue your dreams, you will inevitably spend more and more of your time doing what you enjoy and do best. That's good. You can achieve your dreams only if you focus on your priorities. But success requires something else: discipline. One of the best ways I know to improve discipline is to do something you don't enjoy doing—every day. If you learn to do what you must, you will be able to do what you want.

— John C. Maxwell

$\mathscr{I}$began to have an idea of my life, not as the slow shaping of achievement to fit my preconceived purposes, but as the gradual discovery and growth of a purpose which I did not know.

— Joanna Field

$\mathscr{D}$iamonds are only chunks of coal that stuck to their job, you see.

— Minnie Richard Smith

$\mathscr{O}$ur aspirations are our possibilities.

— Robert Browning

Whatever you can do, or dream you can, begin it.

— Goethe

Do what you can, with what you have, where you are.

—Theodore Roosevelt

All it takes is one idea to solve an impossible problem.

— Robert H. Schuller

The future belongs to those who believe in the beauty of their dreams.

—— Eleanor Roosevelt

Cherish your visions and your dreams as they are the children of your soul; the blueprints of your ultimate achievements.

—— Napoleon Hill

Hope is the thing with feathers that perches in the soul.

—— Emily Dickinson

Following Your Dream

What good is the American Dream if you never follow it? Many people dream and dream, but they never act. For dreams to become reality there must be a conscious plan of action. In a 1986 *Reader's Digest* article, Barbara Bartocci listed six points to consider while searching to find your dream. It seems that many people have a dream but are content to accept whatever comes along. Bartocci says that we must take our dreams seriously. Never believe that you are too old to accomplish something. Col. Harland Sanders began selling his chicken recipe at age sixty-five, and his "new" career lasted twenty-five years. Take on your dream in stages. Make plans to move closer to its reality, one step at a time, breaking each step into small, attainable goals.

—Alan C. Elliott,
Daily Dose of the American Dream

Some people try to do a little bit of everything in the hopes that something will hit pay dirt. Such a lack of focus can hold up your progress. You must pick and choose; you cannot have everything or do everything at once. Do only those things that are really important. Drop all non-productive chores. Be willing not only to change your circumstances, but also to change your thinking and personality. Develop yourself into the individual who can actually be a success in your dream. Finally, refuse to accept "no" for an answer, even from yourself. Yes, you can change. Yes, you can follow your dream.

—Alan C. Elliott,
A Daily Dose of the American Dream

*W*ithout a vision the people perish.

— Proverbs 29:18

*B*e sure you're right, then go ahead.

— Davy Crockett

A day is not ordinary or extra-ordinary in itself. It is ordinary or extra-ordinary depending on how I view it and what I choose to do with it.

— Ruth Senter

$\mathscr{I}$t's important to start . . . start from right where you are.

— Wally Amos

$\mathscr{B}$e ready. Be ready. The time will come.

— Sherri Coale

$\mathscr{T}$here is one thing stronger than all the armies in the world, and that is an idea whose time has come.

— Victor Hugo

To comprehend a man's life, it is necessary to know not merely what he does, but also what he purposely leaves undone. There is a limit to the work that can be got out of a human body or a human brain, and he is a wise man who wastes no energy on pursuits for which he is not fitted; and he is still wiser who, from among the things that he can do well, chooses and resolutely follows the best.

—William E. Gladstone

*T*he secret of success in life is for a man to be ready for his opportunity.

— Benjamin Disraeli

A trip of a thousand miles is begun with a single step.

— Chinese proverb

*F*ar away there in the sunshine are my highest aspirations. I may not reach them, but I can look up and see their beauty, believe in them, and try to follow where they lead.

— Louisa May Alcott

*I*n the long run you hit only what you aim at. Therefore, though you should fail immediately, you had better aim at something high.

— Henry David Thoreau

*T*he shell must break before the bird can fly.

— Alfred, Lord Tennyson

*I*t is not death that a man should fear, but he should fear never beginning to live.

— Marcus Aurelius Antoninus

It is the steady and merciless increase of occupations, the augmented speed at which we are always trying to live, the crowding of each day with more work than it can profitably hold, which has cost us, among other good things, the undisturbed enjoyment of friends. Friendship takes time, and we have no time to give it.

—Agnes Repplier

$\mathcal{E}$ach friend represents a world in us, a world possibly not born until they arrive, and it is only by this meeting that a new world is born.

— Anaïs Nin

$\mathcal{T}$he world is so empty if one thinks only of mountains, rivers, and cities; but to know someone here and there who thinks and feels with us, and who, though distant, is close to us in spirit, this makes the earth an inhabited garden.

— Goethe

*W*hatever you are, be a good one.

— Abraham Lincoln

*W*e're all travelers in the desert of life and the best we can find in our journey is an honest friend.

— Robert Louis Stevenson

*F*riendship is unnecessary, like philosophy, like art . . . It has no survival value; rather it is one of those things that give value to survival.

— C. S. Lewis

*A*ge is not important unless you are a cheese.

— Helen Hayes

*T*ry not to become a person of success but rather a person of value.

—Albert Einstein

*L*ots of people want to ride with you in the limo, but what you want is someone who will take the bus with you when the limo breaks down.

— Oprah Winfrey

The world stands aside to let anyone pass who knows where he is going.

— David Starr Gordon

The will to do, the soul to dare.

— Sir Walter Scott

You will never change your life until you change something you do daily. The secret of your success is found in your daily routine.

— John C. Maxwell

Do all the good you can,
By all the means you can,
In all the ways you can,
In all the places you can,
At all the times you can,
To all the people you can,
As long as ever you can.

— John Wesley

*C*onfidence is the companion to success.

— Anonymous

*I*f you don't know where you're going, you'll end up somewhere else.

—Yogi Berra

*I*f there is any great secret of success in life, it lies in the ability to put yourself in the other person's place and to see things from his point of view—as well as your own.

— Henry Ford

$\mathcal{L}$et us endeavor to live, so that when we die, even the undertaker will be sorry.

— Mark Twain

$\mathcal{F}$riendship is the only cement that will hold the world together.

— Woodrow Wilson

$\mathcal{I}$t is by forgiving that one is forgiven.

— Mother Teresa

*F*riendship with oneself is all-important, because without it one cannot be friends with anyone else in the world.

— Eleanor Roosevelt

A man's reach should exceed his grasp, or what's heaven for?

— Robert Browning

*T*he superior man makes the difficulty to be overcome his first interest; success comes only later.

— Confucius

$\mathscr{I}$t's right to be content with what you have, but not with what you are.

— Anonymous

$\mathscr{W}$hen what we are is what we want to be, that's happiness.

— Malcolm Forbes

$\mathscr{I}$f you walk with God, you can have victory, even when things get really tough. So the challenge is to walk with God.

— David Robinson

And the day came when the risk [it took] to remain tight in the bud was more painful than the risk it took to blossom.

— Anais Nin

You don't need to know all the answers. No one is smart enough yet to ask you all the questions.

— Anonymous

Life is either a daring adventure or nothing.

— Helen Keller

Be glad of life because it gives you the chance to love and to work and to play and to look at the stars.

— Henry Van Dyke

To love deeply in one direction makes us more loving in all others.

— Anne-Sophie Swetchine

Render a service if you would succeed. This is the supreme law of life.

— Henry Miller

*E*verybody can be great . . . because everybody can serve. You don't have to have a college degree to serve. You don't have to make your subject and verb agree to serve. You only need a heart full of grace. A soul generated by love.

— Martin Luther King, Jr.

There is a time for everything,

And a season for every activity under heaven:

A time to be born and a time to die,

A time to plant and a time to uproot,

A time to kill and a time to heal,

A time to tear down and a time to build,

A time to weep and a time to laugh,

A time to mourn and a time to dance,

A time to scatter stones and a time to gather them,

A time to embrace and a time to refrain,

A time to search and a time to give up,

A time to keep and a time to throw away,

A time to tear and a time to mend,

A time to be silent and a time to speak,

A time to love and a time to hate,

A time for war and a time for peace.

— Ecclesiastes 3:1-8

*W*inning the prize [1963 Nobel Prize in physics] wasn't half as exciting as doing the work itself.

— Maria Goeppert Mayer

*E*very problem carries the seed of an equivalent or greater benefit.

— Zig Ziglar

*S*mall opportunities are often the beginning of great enterprises.

— Demosthenes

*I*t is no use to wait for your ship to come in unless you have sent one out.

— Belgian proverb

*A*mbition's a good thing if you've got it headed in the right direction.

— Josh White

*A*nd let us not grow weary while doing good, for in due season we shall reap if we do not lose heart.

— Galatians 6:9

*D*on't confuse fame with success. Madonna is one; Helen Keller is the other.

— Erma Bombeck

*S*uccess usually comes to those who are too busy to be looking for it.

— Henry David Thoreau

*A*n aim in life is the only fortune worth finding.

— Robert Louis Stevenson

Do more than exist: live.

Do more than touch: feel.

Do more than look: observe.

Do more than read: absorb.

Do more than hear: listen.

Do more than listen: understand.

Do more than think: reflect.

Do more than just talk: say something.

— Anonymous

*M*arie Curie didn't stumble upon radium by accident. She searched and experimented and sweated and suffered years before she found it. Success rarely is an accident.

— B. C. Forbes

*B*y perseverance the snail reached the ark.

— Charles Spurgeon

*W*e make a living by what we get, we make a life by what we give.

—Winston Churchill

*N*ever give up then, for that is just the place and time that the tide will turn.

— Harriet Beecher Stowe

*S*uccess seems to be connected with action. Successful people keep moving. They make mistakes, but they don't quit.

— Conrad Hilton

*C*ourage and perseverance have a magical talisman, before which difficulties disappear and obstacles vanish into air.

— John Quincy Adams

Attitude is more important than the past, than education, than money, than circumstances. Every day we have a choice regarding the attitude we will embrace for that day.

— Charles Swindoll

High Expectations

In his book *Secrets of Successful Selling,* John Murphy relates the story of the man who could make only $5,000 a year. No matter what situation the man was in, he believed he was a $5,000-a-year employee. When he was given a good sales territory, he made $5,000. In a bad territory, he made $5,000. Once, he made $5,000 early in the year and was sick for the rest of the year, although doctors could not determine why. Luckily, the salesman finally got the message that it was his limited belief in himself that was holding him back. He needed to raise his expectations and have a more positive dream of what he could accomplish.

—Alan C. Elliott,
Daily Dose of the American Dream

Do not keep the alabaster boxes of your love and tenderness sealed up until your friends are dead. Fill their lives with sweetness. Speak approvingly cheering words while their ears can hear them and while their hearts can be thrilled by them.

— George W. Childs

A genuine friend encourages and challenges us to live out our best thoughts, honor our purest motives, and achieve our most significant dreams.

— Dan Reiland

*S*uccess doesn't come to you. You go to it.

— Marva Collins

*M*ountains cannot be surmounted except by winding paths.

— Goethe

*C*haracter cannot be developed in ease and quiet. Only through experience of trial and suffering can the soul be strengthened, vision cleared, ambition inspired, and success achieved.

— Helen Keller

There is no substitute for experience, and the more you learn to react properly under pressure, the better you'll be able to perform the next time.

— Byron Nelson

Success is spelled w-o-r-k.

— Robert H. Schuller

Things don't turn up in this world until somebody turns them up.

— James Garfield

*P*erseverance is not a long race; it is many short races one after another.

—Walter Elliot

*P*ersistence is the twin sister of excellence. One is a matter of quality; the other, a matter of time.

— Marabel Morgan

*G*enius produces great ideas and concepts. Hard work produces results.

— Zig Ziglar

The True Measure of Success

To be able to carry money without spending it;

To be able to bear an injustice without retaliating;

To be able to do one's duty when critical eyes watch;

To be able to keep at a job until it is finished;

To be able to do the work and let others receive the recognition;

To be able to accept criticism without letting it whip you;

To like those who push you down;

To love when hate is all around you;

To follow God when others put detour signs in your path;

To have a peace of heart and mind because you have given God your best.

This is the true measure of success.

— Anonymous

*T*here is no substitute for hard work. Genius is one percent inspiration and ninety-nine percent perspiration.

—Thomas Edison

*T*here might be false starts and do-overs. You are entitled to experiment before you find your calling.

— Jane Pauley

*I*f you throw enough spaghetti against the wall, some of it is going to stick.

— Joe Girard

𝒢enius, that power which dazzles humans, is oft but perseverance in disguise.

— H. W. Austin

𝒟etermine that the thing can and shall be done, and then we shall find the way.

— Abraham Lincoln

𝒟on't dodge difficulties, meet them, greet them, beat them. All great men have been through the wringer.

— A. A. Milne

You can't weep or talk your way through a mess. When you come up against a problem, you have to work your way through it.

— Marva Collins

The difference between mediocrity and greatness is extra effort.

— George Allen

When you have exhausted all the possibilities, remember this: You haven't.

— Robert H. Schuller

Whatsoever thy hand findeth to do, do it with all thy might.

— Ecclesiastes 9:10

It's not what you take with you but what you leave behind that defines greatness.

— Edward Gardner

Real wisdom is looking at the world from God's point of view.

— Mary Crowley

$\mathscr{I}$t is the surmounting of difficulties that makes heroes.

— Lajos Kossuth

$\mathscr{M}$any strokes, though with a little axe, hew down and fell
the hardest-timbered oak.

—WilliamShakespeare

$\mathscr{T}$he person who works diligently toward a dream, and keeps
his focus on the goal, will wake up some fine morning and
realize that he has achieved what he has dreamed.

—Alan C. Elliott

The only way the magic works is by hard work.

— Jim Henson

Are you in earnest? Seize this very minute. What you can do or think you can, begin it.

— Goethe

The great thing and the hard thing is to stick to things when you have outlived the first interest, and not yet got the second, which comes with a sort of mastery.

— Janet Erskine Stuart

You don't just luck into things as much as you'd like to think you do. You build step by step, whether it's friendships or opportunities.

— Barbara Bush

Friendship is the inexpressible comfort of feeling safe with a person, having neither to weigh thoughts or measure words.

— George Eliot

Deal as gently with the faults of others as you do with your own.

— Chinese proverb

The better part of one's life consists of his friendships.

—Abraham Lincoln

Friendship is like money, easier made than kept.

— Samuel Butler

A friend is one to whom one can pour out all the contents of one's heart, chaff and grain together, knowing that the gentlest of hands will take and sift it, keep what is worth keeping, and, with the breath of kindness, blow the rest away.

—Arabian proverb

*I*f one advances confidently in the direction of his dreams
and endeavors to live the life which he imagined, he will meet
with success unexpected in common hours.

— Henry David Thoreau

*T*alk not of wasted affection; affection never was wasted.

— Henry Wadsworth Longfellow

*I*t is a fine seasoning for joy to think of those we love.

— Molière

*W*isdom is the right use of knowledge. To know is not to be wise. Many men know a great deal, and are all the greater fools for it. There is no fool so great as a knowing fool. But to know how to use knowledge is to have wisdom.

— Charles H. Spurgeon

$\mathcal{T}$is the set of the sail that decides the goal, and not the storms of life.

— Ella Wheeler Wilcox

$\mathcal{P}$ut your knowledge to practical experience and reap the harvest.

— A.A. Milne

A Gift Left in the Case

$\mathcal{N}$iccolo Paganini is considered one of the greatest violinists of all time. He was a virtuoso, performing his first concert at age eleven. His great technical ability revolutionized violin technique across Europe.

When he died in 1840, he willed his violin to Genoa, Italy, the place of his birth. But he did so upon one condition: that no other artist ever play his instrument again. Glad to have the violin come into their possession, the city's fathers agreed to the request, and they put it in a beautiful case for everyone to see.

But wooden instruments have a certain peculiarity. As long as they are handled, they show no wear. But if one lies unused, it begins to decay, which is what happened to Paganini's violin. His once-exquisite instrument became worm-eaten and useless. Other violins of the same vintage have been handed down through the generations, from one gifted musician to another, and they continue to bring great music to attentive audiences. But Paganini's violin is a crumbling relic of what it once was.

The talent you have been given by God cannot be set aside like Paganini's violin. If you do not nurture your ability, it will decay until it is useless. But if you consistently work with it, diligently trying to bring out its best, it will bring forth "music" that will not only give you joy, but will also serve others and bring you success.

— John C. Maxwell

$\mathcal{L}$et your intentions be good, embodied in good thoughts, cheerful words, and unselfish deeds, and the world will be to you a bright and happy place in which you can work and play and serve.

— Grenville Kleiser

*I*magination is more important than knowledge.

— Albert Einstein

*L*ife is like a grindstone: Whether is grinds you down or pol-
ishes you up depends on what you're made of.

— Anonymous

*I*t is the creative potential itself in human beings that is the
image of God.

— Mary Daly

$\mathscr{T}$he man who insists upon seeing with perfect clearness before he decides, never decides.

— Henri-Frederic Amiel

$\mathscr{W}$hat is required is sight and insight. Then you might add one more: excite.

— Robert Frost

$\mathscr{Y}$ou never really lose until you quit trying.

— Mike Ditka

$\mathcal{P}$eople can block you.

Friends can overprotect you.

Forces may frustrate you.

Enemies may obstruct you.

Families may discourage you.

But only you and you alone can defeat yourself.

— Robert H. Schuller

A person is persuaded more by the depth of your convictions than by the breadth of your knowledge.

— Zig Ziglar

To be what we are, and to become what we are capable of becoming, is the only end of life.

— Robert Louis Stevenson

Never grow a wishbone, daughter, where a backbone ought to be.

— Clementine Paddleford

*C*ommon sense is instinct, and enough of it is genius.

— George Bernard Shaw

*F*or they can conquer who believe they can.

—Virgil

I have found that the men and women who got to the top were those who did the job they had in hand with everything they had of energy, enthusiasm, and hard work.

— Harry Truman

*W*e can do anything we want to do if we stick with it long enough.

— Helen Keller

*T*ake time to deliberate, but when the time for action arrives, stop thinking and go in.

— Andrew Jackson

*A*ttention is the stuff that memory is made of, and memory is accumulated genius.

— J. R. Lowell

With ordinary talent and extraordinary perseverance, all
things are attainable.

— Thomas Buxton

Wisdom . . . is more precious than jewels, and nothing you
desire compares with her.

— Proverbs 8:11

Learn from the mistakes of others. You can't live long
enough to make them all yourself.

— Martin Vanbee

Lemons to Lemonade

The person with an easy life is the exception rather than the rule. At some point in life, most people find themselves in a state of depression or on the edge of ruin. This may be the very time when something wonderful can happen. It is often when we hit our lowest point, when we have nothing else to lose, that we are willing to take those risks that we would otherwise deem to be too foolish or too dangerous. Adversity may bring out the best in us. John Bunyan wrote the classic *Pilgrim's Progress* after being imprisoned for his religious beliefs. O. Henry (William Sydney Porter), the great short story writer, discovered his writing talent while in prison. Charles Dickens had a tragic first romance and, drawing on his personal life experience, produced the story of David Copperfield.

Beethoven was deaf, Milton was blind, and Helen Keller was deaf, mute, and blind. Yet, their contributions to the world live on. These people with severe handicaps became overcomers. Life had given them little, but they made the most of what they had. Perhaps you will not face these particular handicaps. However, what if you were fired or laid off? What if you were to lose a loved one or all of your wealth? What if you were physically or emotionally handicapped? Consider how much you could contribute to the world if you pushed aside those things that are holding you back. Can you, like those individuals mentioned above, overcome your shortcomings and release the power of your talents?

—Alan C. Elliott,
A Daily Dose of the American Dream

All progress, all achievement is the story of imagination.

— A. B. ZuTavern

Practice makes perfect.

— Proverb

I do the very best I know how, the very best I can, and I mean to keep on doing so until the end.

— Abraham Lincoln

$\mathcal{P}$roblems are only opportunities in work clothes.

— Henry J. Kaiser

$\mathcal{Y}$ou can become the star of the hour if you make the minutes count.

—Anonymous

$\mathcal{T}$he supreme happiness of life is the conviction of being loved for yourself, or more correctly, being loved in spite of yourself.

—Victor Hugo

$\mathcal{S}$uccess is not measured by what a man accomplishes, but by the opposition he has encountered, and the courage with which he has maintained the struggle against overwhelming odds.

— Charles Lindbergh

*I*f enough people think of a thing and work hard enough at it, I guess it's pretty nearly bound to happen, wind and weather permitting.

— Laura Ingalls Wilder

*E*verything yields to diligence.

— Antiphanes

The art of living rightly is like all arts: it must be learned and practiced with incessant care.

— Goethe

Confidence brings joy when we fix our attention on the things for which we are thankful.

— Charles Swindoll

The greatest wealth is to live content with little.

— Plato

*T*o laugh often and much;

To win the respect of intelligent people and the affection of children;

To earn the appreciation of honest critics

And endure the betrayal of false friends;

To appreciate beauty, to find the best in others;

To leave the world a bit better whether by a healthy child, a garden
patch, or a redeemed social condition;

To know even one life has breathed easier because you have lived.

This is to have succeeded.

— Ralph Waldo Emerson

$\mathscr{B}$e not angry that you cannot make others as you wish them to be, since you cannot make yourself as you wish to be.

—Thomas à Kempis

$\mathscr{W}$ithout perseverance talent is a barren bed.

—Welsh proverb

*L*ife is not easy for any of us. But what of that? We must have perseverance and, above all, confidence in ourselves. We must believe that we are gifted for something, and that this thing, at whatever cost, must be attained.

— Marie Curie

A man watches his pear tree day after day, impatient for the ripening of the fruit. Let him attempt to force the process, and he may spoil both fruit and tree. But let him patiently wait, and the ripe fruit at length falls into his lap.

— Abraham Lincoln

*P*atience is a necessary ingredient of genius.

— Benjamin Disraeli

*W*isely and slow; they stumble that run fast.

—William Shakespeare

All things come to him who waits—provided he knows what he is waiting for.

—Woodrow Wilson

The greatest mistake made in timing is impatience. The lesson of patience must be learned loud and clear, again and again, in the process of success.

—Robert H. Schuller

I have learned that success is to be measured not so much by the position that one has reached in life as by the obstacles which he has overcome while trying to succeed.

— Booker T. Washington

I t is easier to go down a hill than up, but the view is best from the top.

— Arnold Bennett

A life is not important except in the impact it has on others.

— Jackie Robinson

*P*roblems produce patience; patience produces persistence; persistence produces character; character produces hope; hope produces power.

— Zig Ziglar

Adopt the pace of nature, her secret is patience.

— Ralph Waldo Emerson

Whoever wants to reach a distant goal must take many small steps.

— Helmut Schmidt

Be kind, for everyone you meet is fighting a harder battle.

— Plato

There was a definite process by which one made people into friends, and it involved talking to them and listening to them for hours at a time.

— Rebecca West

Do not " . . . be indifferent to the joys and beauties of this life. For through these, as through pain, we are enabled to see purpose in randomness, pattern in chaos. We do not have to understand in order to believe that behind the mystery and the fascination there is love."

— Madeleine L'Engle

*B*eware of the barrenness of an overcrowded life.

— Anonymous

*A*im above morality. Be not simply good, be good for something.

— Henry David Thoreau

*I*t is not what comes into a man's hands that enriches him but what he saves from slipping through them.

— H. F. Kletzing

$\mathscr{W}$hen values are clear, decisions are easy.

— Roy Disney

$\mathscr{I}$t's not how much we have, but how much we enjoy what we have, that makes for happiness.

— Charles Spurgeon

$\mathscr{I}$ find the great thing in this world is not so much where we stand as in what direction we are going.

— Oliver Wendell Holmes

Success is going from failure to failure without losing your enthusiasm.

— Abraham Lincoln

Far better it is to dare mighty things, to win glorious triumphs, even though checkered with failure, than to take rank with those poor spirits who neither enjoy much nor suffer much because they live in the gray twilight that knows not victory or defeat.

— Theodore Roosevelt

Wisdom outweighs any wealth.

— Sophocles

The way to success and a broad, beautiful outlook on life
more often than not leads over obstacles and up a steep climb
before we reach the hilltop.

— Laura Ingalls Wilder

The fear of the Lord is the beginning of wisdom,
And knowledge of the Holy one is understanding.

— Proverbs 9:10

*M*anage your time, and you'll manage to succeed in accomplishing what appear to be impossible goals.

— Robert H. Schuller

*S*weetie, you just cannot judge a book by its cover.

— Thelma Wells

*H*umble people don't think less of themselves; they just think of themselves less.

— Zig Ziglar

A joy shared is a joy doubled.

— Goethe

*D*o unto others as you would have them do unto you.

— Matthew 7:5

*T*he greatest need in the world today is for people of sweet dispositions, good character, and harmonious nature.

— Pearl Buck

$\mathcal{T}$ake calculated risks. That is quite different from being rash.

— Gen. George S. Patton

$\mathcal{B}$e true to your highest conviction.

—William Ellery Channing

$\mathcal{S}$ix essential qualities that are the key to success: sincerity, personal integrity, humility, courtesy, wisdom, charity.

— Dr. William Menninger

*T*il it has loved, no man or woman can become itself.

— Emily Dickinson

*T*he real secret of happiness is not what you give or what you receive; it's what you share.

—Anonymous

*N*o one is useless in this world who lightens the burden of it to anyone.

— Charles Dickens

Courage is the first of human qualities because it is the quality which guarantees all the others.

—Winston Churchill

He who moves not forward goes backward.

— Goethe

Courage is resistance to fear, mastery of fear—not absence of fear.

— Mark Twain

$\mathcal{O}$ne is not born into the world to do everything, but to do something.

— Henry David Thoreau

$\mathcal{T}$he talent of success is nothing more than doing what you can do well and doing well whatever you do without thought of fame.

— Henry Wadsworth Longfellow

$\mathcal{I}$ long to accomplish a great and noble task; but it is my chief duty and job to accomplish humble tasks as though they were great and noble. The world is moved along, not only by the mighty shoves of its heroes, but also by the aggregate of the tiny pushes of each honest worker.

— Helen Keller

Stopping to know what you're doing and why isn't a one-time activity. It must be a daily activity. Spend time every morning or evening to think about the coming day. Set aside a day twelve times a year to plan your month. And spend one whole week each year reflecting and evaluating, to measure the year that's passed, to plan the year that's coming, and to stay on track with your purpose.

— John C. Maxwell

𝒩othing gives one person so much advantage over another as to remain cool and unruffled under all circumstances.

——Thomas Jefferson

𝒢reat tranquility of heart is his who cares for neither praise nor blame.

——Thomas à Kempis

ℛeason and judgment are the qualities of a leader.

——Tacitus

$\mathcal{T}$he language of excitement is at best picturesque. You must be calm before you can utter oracles.

— Henry David Thoreau

$\mathcal{T}$he effort is what counts in everything.

— John Wooden

$\mathcal{P}$ossess your soul with patience.

— John Dryden

A happy family is but an earlier heaven.

— Sir John Browning

Usually, when the distractions of daily life deplete our energy, the first thing we eliminate is the thing we need the most: quiet, reflective time. Time to dream, time to think, time to contemplate what's working and what's not, so that we can make changes for the better.

— Sarah Ban Breathnach

$\mathcal{G}$ive others a chance—you never know what they will become!

— Heather Whitestone

$\mathcal{H}$ave patience and the mulberry leaf will become satin.

— Spanish proverb

$\mathcal{I}$t's where we go, and what we do when we get there, that tells us who we are.

— Joyce Carol Oates

There are two types of people who never achieve much in their lifetime. The person who won't do what he is told, and the person who does no more than he is told.

— Andrew Carnegie

To experience happiness we must live in this moment, savor it for what it is, not running ahead in anticipation of some future date nor lagging behind in paralysis of the past.

— Luci Swindoll

$\mathcal{A}$ big achievement is made up of little steps.

— Robert H. Schuller

$\mathcal{T}$he life that is unexamined is not worth living.

— Plato

$\mathcal{C}$almness can lay great errors to rest.

— Ecclesiastes 10: 4

*I*t is not length of life, but depth of life.

— Ralph Waldo Emerson

*O*ur deepest fear is not that we are inadequate. Our deepest fear is that we are powerful beyond measure. It is our light, not our darkness, that most frightens us. We ask ourselves, "Who am I to be brilliant, gorgeous, talented, and famous?" Actually, who're you not to be? You are a child of God."

— Nelson Mandela

A wife of noble character who can find?

She is worth far more than rubies.

Her husband has full confidence in her and lacks

nothing of value.

She brings him good, not harm, all the days of

her life . . .

She speaks with wisdom, and faithful instruction

is on her tongue.

She watches over the affairs of her household . . .

Her children arise and call her blessed; her husband

also, and he praises her:

Many women do noble things, but you surpass

them all.

— Proverbs 31: 10-12

*W*hoso loves believes the impossible.

— Elizabeth Barrett Browning

*M*y little children, let us not love in word or in tongue, but in deed and in truth.

— I John 3:18

*W*e love because it is the only true adventure.

— Nikki Giovanni, poet

My grandfather once told me that there are two kinds of people: those who work and those who take the credit. He told me to try to be in the first group; there was less competition there.

— Indira Gandhi

I once complained to my father that I didn't seem to be able to do things the same way other people did. Dad's advice? "Margo, don't be a sheep. People hate sheep. They eat sheep."

— Margo Kaufman

*I*t's really important that, as women, we tell our stories. That is what helps seed our imaginations.

— Ann Bancroft

*T*he most important thing that parents can teach their children is how to get along without them.

— Frank A. Clark

*O*h, how immensely important is this work of preparing the daughters of the land to be good mothers!

— Mary Lyon